# LINE?

## The Creative Way
## for Actors
## to Quickly Memorize
## Monologues
## and
## Dialogues

*"Bottom line, the memory techniques taught in LINE? work. Any actor who's ever struggled to remember their lines needs to buy this book and read it right away. I only wish I learned this memorization method years ago."*

Javier Molina
Associate Director of the Action Theatre Conservatory
and Lifetime Member of the Actors Studio
●●●●●●●●

*"Actors and actresses, young and old, can now throw out the old methods of rote memorization. Kelner has crafted LINE? in a way that leverages your creative mind and gracefully marries proven memorization methods with the actor's natural imaginative instincts which results in faster line memorization. This resource is a must for every actor who wants to improve their ability to memorize their lines."*

Jamie Nast
Author of Idea Mapping: How to Access Your Hidden Brain Power, Learn Faster, Remember More, and Achieve Success in Business
●●●●●●●●

*"Whether you're a novice cast in a community theatre production or a professional actor whose Teflon brain is causing you to lose jobs, LINE? will save your life. This is the best monologue and dialogue memorization system that I have ever come across. Jared Kelner breaks the process down into simple steps that will help you memorize your lines quickly and creatively. I am highly recommending this book to the students I teach and the actors I direct."*

Gerry Appel
Director of The Playhouse Acting Academy
●●●●●●●●

# LINE?

## The Creative Way
## for Actors
## to Quickly Memorize
## Monologues
## and
## Dialogues

**Jared Kelner**

Title: LINE?

Subtitle: The Creative Way for Actors to Quickly Memorize
Monologues and Dialogues

Publisher: The Infinite Mind Training Group
www.memory-trainers.com

Author: Jared Kelner
www.jaredkelner.com

Editor: Cynthia Willett Sherwood from Second Set of Eyes
www.secondsetofeyes.com

Cover Art: Rantilini S. from Rantistic
www.rantistic.zzl.org

ISBN - 10: 0-9826558-3-5
ISBN - 13: 978-0-9826558-3-2

First Edition, 2012

Published in the United States of America

*To Debbie, Coby, and Tori for your unconditional love and support*

*To Eric Morace and Corey Nathan for your artistic inspiration*

# TABLE OF CONTENTS

# INTRODUCTION

If you're like most actors, at one point in your career you've struggled with memorizing your lines. Perhaps you couldn't remember the next part of your monologue, or maybe the next line of dialogue just wasn't coming to you. The sad fact is that most actors fail to use their natural imaginative abilities that can help them memorize their lines quickly and instead rely on repetitive, rote memorization techniques to force the text into their brains.

You may have tried some of the following monotonous memory methods: highlighting your lines and covering them with another piece of paper; recording the other person's lines into a tape recorder and talking during the paused recording; writing the cue line and your line on opposite sides of a note card and flipping them over; writing your lines on sticky notes and pasting them around the set; repeating your lines again and again while exercising; or even playing a recording of your lines over and over while you sleep, hoping that your subconscious mind will magically absorb the dialogue. These methods all rely on rote memorization through stale repetition.

When actors use these methods, they're working against their nature as imaginative and creative souls. Actors inherently and instinctively have vivid imaginations. They're creative forces who see the gray world in bright colors. By leveraging their artistic nature and unique vision, actors can accelerate the memorization process.

So put down the highlighter. Turn off the tape recorder. Throw away the note cards. Instead, turn on your imagination and tap into the unbounded world of your creative mind; your lines will be quickly learned, easily memorized, and instantly recalled. Oh, and by the way, the creative approach to memorizing lines is fun.

# SECTION 1: THE BASICS

## BENCHMARK CHALLENGE

By the time you finish this book, your memory skills should have grown significantly. To determine how much of an improvement there is, it's important to establish a baseline of where your skills are right now. Most people get stressed when they hear they have to take a test, so to keep your heart rate down, this next section is called a "Benchmark Challenge."

It's simple: just read and memorize the list of ten items below in sixty seconds. Remembering the list is critical, but remembering it in the correct order is equally important. Think about this list like it's a monologue. If you delivered your lines out of order, you'd be doing a disservice to the playwright and you'd likely confuse the audience. The same principle holds true with this Benchmark Challenge. The order is just as important as the information.

Take a deep breath. Be honest and allow yourself a maximum of sixty seconds to memorize the list below. Ready. Set. Go:

### Benchmark Challenge List
1. The Mona Lisa
2. "For Sale" sign
3. Brick building
4. The Nobel Prize
5. Two boxers with arms raised
6. Rainbow
7. Frying pan
8. Mountain
9. Hamster wheel
10. Confetti

57. 58. 59. 60, and stop. Very good. In a few minutes you'll be asked to recall the list, but for now it's important to continue reading the next chapter, *Facts about Memory*. Before we see just how well you can recall the list and its order, we must first establish a common vocabulary about the memorization process and how your brain recalls information.

# FACTS ABOUT MEMORY

Our mind thinks in pictures, not in words. I'll prove it to you. If I write the word elephant, you don't simply picture the letters e-l-e-p-h-a-n-t. Rather, you see an image of an elephant in your mind. You picture a large gray animal with big floppy ears and a long trunk. If I write the word fireworks, again, you don't picture the letters f-i-r-e-w-o-r-k-s. You picture a night sky—probably on the 4th of July or at the county fair—and see glorious explosions of red and yellow and green and blue and white and orange and purple and green. (By the way, are you thinking of *Joseph and the Amazing Technicolor Dreamcoat*? If you weren't, you probably are now.)

Again, our mind thinks in pictures, never just in words. This is the main reason why actors struggle with remembering their lines, because they're trying to memorize words on a page and our mind doesn't think in letters and words. As a side note, this is also why many people have trouble remembering people's names. It's because names are just words, not images, and until you turn the name into an image—such as a microphone for a guy named Mike—and do something with that image, you'll struggle to remember someone's name. In this book, we'll go into great detail about the process of turning words into images and then leveraging those images to quickly and easily remember your lines.

One important note about this book: there are no pictures and that's by design. As you learn and apply the techniques presented, it's critical that you create images from your mind and from your imagination. We don't want to give you any images to work with, because that would only slow down your progress. The faster you create images for yourself, the stronger the techniques will take root and your results will be amazing.

Another important fact about memory is that interest in the material being memorized plays an important role in how easily that information is memorized. A perfect example would be an avid theatre fan who can instantly recall the names of every play that has appeared on Broadway over the last decade, but when asked to remember the quadratic equation to solve a math problem, he can't even recall where to begin. In this example, the names of the plays are quickly remembered because this individual has a high level of interest in the theatre, but solving an algebraic equation is nothing that interests him.

Another example is when you can remember every line to a song or a movie because it holds a fond memory or because you have some emotional connection to it. Politics is another subject that demonstrates the principle of why interest is important in memorization. If you're asked to recall the Declaration of Independence, you probably struggle to remember anything more than the first few lines ("We hold these truths to be self evident..." Actually, that line is from the second sentence. It starts with,

"When in the course of human events…," but if you didn't know that, it's because the Declaration of Independence doesn't hold a high interest level for you). So to recall information easily, you must have interest in the material *and* you must first see the information in the form of an image, not just the plain text.

The third fact about your memory is that we tend to forget the everyday mundane things in life, but we quickly remember information and events that are unusual or emotional. Stop for a moment and think about the last time you passed a car on the side of the road while driving on the highway. Usually, it's difficult to recall details about that car because it's such an ordinary occurrence; driving past a car on the shoulder creates little interest because it happens frequently enough that you pay little attention to it. However, if you were stuck in traffic on the highway due to an accident, as you drove past the wreckage, even traveling at twenty miles per hour, you'd easily be able to retell the events to someone else if you saw that the car was totaled or on fire. You'd remember if there was a fire truck, an ambulance, and police cars. You'd be able to tell people if you saw anyone on a stretcher, if there was blood, if there was glass on the ground, if people were panicked, if there was a fire, if there were people crying, and so on.

You can see these images vividly because they don't happen every day. They're anything but mundane. They're packed with emotion, and even if it were years later, you'd probably be able to recall most of the images you saw that day. When an event is full of action, excitement, or emotion and it's something that doesn't happen every day (meaning it's not mundane), you can quickly recall the information.

It's also important to point out that people have different ways to absorb information. We take in data through our senses. We see things, we hear things, we taste things, we smell things, and we feel things. People remember information by accessing memories based on one or more of these senses. If you were asked to speak the words of *The Star Spangled Banner*, you'd probably mess up the words shortly after you began. But if you sing it, the words would flow much easier, without mistakes. Why is this? It's because the association of the words to the melody is such a strong bond that when it's broken, your mind struggles to recall the information.

Another example is a musical theatre actor who can easily remember the lyrics to all of his songs, but who struggles to remember the spoken dialogue between the other characters. Or think about when you're driving and a song comes on the radio that you haven't heard in twenty years. The moment the lead singer starts to sing, you know every word instantly. The lyrics were somewhere in your brain all along, just waiting for you to access them by triggering the association of the melody.

So how does this same principle apply to our other senses? How many times have you seen someone who looked like someone else you know? Or maybe that person looks like a celebrity and when you see him or her, you think about a movie the celebrity was in. That's a visual association. Maybe you're out to dinner and the comfort food you're eating reminds you of a dish your grandmother used to make when you were a child. As you taste the food, you recall your grandparents' house and then memories of your grandparents rush into your mind. That's an association through taste.

Smell is another very strong stimulus for recalling memories. The sweet scent of a perfume could trigger the image of a long-lost love. Or perhaps the smell of farm animals as you drive through the rural part of town may take you back to a time you spent working with cows or horses.

The last sense is touch, which may be associated to a certain movement or physical action. For example, a little boy who touches a hot stove and gets burned will always remember that touching the red coils or the flame results in pain. Another type of movement that triggers memory is dance. Just as you as an actor need to remember your lines, a dancer needs to remember the choreography in order to perform the piece correctly. One dance step links to the next and then the next. Before you know it, you're dancing in *Swan Lake*. Your five senses are critical in the memorization process.

The concept of time also plays a significant role in our ability to recall information. Often, when we study for an exam or we attend a lecture, we have an easier time remembering the information that's presented at the start and the end, but we struggle to recall data from the middle. There's a reason for this—when a learning session begins, our mind is fresh and we're focused on actively listening and absorbing the information being presented. As time goes on, our mind sometimes drifts, we get distracted, and our attention isn't as focused as it was when the learning session began. Once we become aware that a break is coming or that the lecture is ending, our attention level picks back up and we become more focused on listening and understanding the information. You can leverage this natural human characteristic for retaining more information at the beginning and end of a learning session. Say, for instance, you have an exam and cram for five uninterrupted hours the night before. That only gives you one beginning and one end. But if you break that study session up into manageable chunks of time, such as five one-hour sessions, when you're done, you'll have created five starts and five finishes.

Simply by using the natural way our brain works, taking breaks will help you recall more information. This also applies to actors trying to memorize their lines. Reading the script over and over and over without taking breaks is much less effective than breaking up the sessions into manageable blocks of time with multiple breaks in between. The more starts and finishes there are, the more information you'll remember, simply by taking advantage of how the brain naturally remembers.

Even more important than the memory concepts we've already discussed is this—in order to remember something new, you must associate it to something you already know. In other words, you must mentally link what you're trying to remember to something that's already locked in your brain. That way, when you think about the old information, the new information will come along with it. This is an abstract concept now, but as we progress through the memory techniques presented in this book, you'll quickly learn just how true this statement is and how easy it is to make the associations stick.

Before continuing, it's important to point out that the memory techniques shared in this book have been around since ancient Rome and Greece. For centuries, creative association memory techniques have been used around the world to help millions of people recall information of all kinds. What this book offers is a customized framework to apply these time-tested and proven techniques in order to help actors remember their lines. To learn more about other applications of memory techniques and how the process can help you in every aspect of your life, please refer to the *Additional Resources* section at the end of this book. There you'll find the best material available today from some of the world's most respected memory experts.

The time has come to see how well you can recall the list of ten items from the Benchmark Challenge. Remember that you must recall all ten items in their correct sequence in order to truly establish your current memory level. Do not cheat. Do not look back or turn the page forward. Just focus on the blank lines below and do your best to either write them down or simply say them out loud.

## Benchmark Challenge List

1. _____
2. _____
3. _____
4. _____
5. _____
6. _____
7. _____
8. _____
9. _____
10. _____

Turn the page to see how well you did.

## Benchmark Challenge List

1. The Mona Lisa
2. "For Sale" sign
3. Brick building
4. The Nobel Prize
5. Two boxers with arms raised
6. Rainbow
7. Frying pan
8. Mountain
9. Hamster wheel
10. Confetti

How did you do? Did you get all ten in the correct order? If you did, then you're starting from a wonderful place (and you've probably had some memory training, whether you know it or not). You'll still learn a tremendous amount from this book, so don't stop reading now. If you didn't remember all ten items in their correct order, don't be discouraged. The average person, after a short break like you had, remembers three to five words in order out of the ten. By the end of this book, you'll be able to recall information forward, backward, and in random order. In fact, your memory skills will be so good that people might call you a genius.

On the line below (or on a separate sheet of paper if you are reading an electronic version), write down how many items you remembered from the list above. You'll come back to this page when you reach the last section of the book to reflect on how much you've learned and grown.

Date: _____

I remembered _____ items from the Benchmark Challenge List.

The last concept to discuss before we dive into specific memory techniques to help you remember your lines is the "Ball of Wax" theory. Picture a ball of wax sitting on top of your head. It's secure and stays there without falling off regardless of where you go or what you do. Imagine that this ball of wax is filled with information—stuff you generally understand and concepts or theories you've learned, but have yet to experience firsthand. In this case, the ball of wax is merely data or raw information, but if you start applying the information and heat up that ball of wax, it melts and drips down your scalp. The moment you feel the hot wax dripping down your forehead and the back of your neck is when you turn the information into knowledge. Once you have knowledge, you begin to grow. Learning concepts, techniques, and theories about memory improvement is important, but applying that information and turning it into experiences and into knowledge is when your abilities improve.

Right now, we're going to pack that ball of wax on top of your head with a lot of information. It's important that you don't judge the ideas. Don't dismiss the concepts at face value. Certainly don't judge yourself as you're learning. If you're going to judge anything, judge the results and your incredible memory skills after you've applied all of the techniques shared in this book. By that time, you'll have melted your ball of wax and will have an arsenal of memory skills in your Actor's Toolbox that can be used to help you easily remember your monologues, dialogues, audition sides, blocking, and anything else you can imagine. As for the silly list of ten things above, we'll get back to that later in the book and when we do, you'll be amazed how ten seemingly unrelated items turn into a powerful technique for remembering a monologue.

●●●●●●●●

# SECTION 2:
# FOUNDATION MEMO TECHNIQUES
## THE LINK AND CHAIN METHOD

In the previous chapter you learned that in order to remember something new, you must associate it to something that you already know. In other words, the first step is to create a story, an association, a link, or a chain that mentally glues or connects the information you're trying to remember to something that you can easily recall. Then, when you think about the old information, the new thing that you're trying to remember will come forward and instantly jump into your mind. Right now we're filling your ball of wax with data that you'll soon apply. In a short while, you'll move from basic understanding to applied knowledge. The concepts may be abstract now, but will become crystal clear in a few minutes.

We'll apply this first technique to help you remember the complete list of Shakespeare's comedies in alphabetical order. This list is probably something that most actors don't know, but should. Why would any actor *not* want to know more about Shakespeare's plays? Take a minute to read the list of plays below, and just as you did with the Mona Lisa Benchmark Challenge, try to remember this list using whatever method you would normally use.

## Shakespeare's Comedies

- All's Well That Ends Well
- As You Like It
- The Comedy of Errors
- Love's Labour's Lost
- Measure for Measure
- The Merchant of Venice
- The Merry Wives of Windsor
- A Midsummer Night's Dream
- Much Ado About Nothing
- The Taming of the Shrew
- The Tempest
- Twelfth Night
- The Two Gentlemen of Verona
- The Winter's Tale

11

For those familiar with Shakespeare's plays, you may have noticed that Troilus and Cressida, Pericles Prince of Tyre, and Cymbeline were omitted from the list. There are different opinions about how to classify these plays, so to avoid confusion they have been left out. If you wish to include them, apply the principles taught below to the three plays when you've finished the chapter.

Test yourself. Close the book for a moment and see if you can say all fourteen plays in order out loud. Do that now. Remember, without experiencing the process, the information will remain inside the ball of wax on top of your head. Our objective is to melt that ball of wax so you have knowledge that can be applied to your monologues and dialogues. Close the book now and say the plays out loud.

●●●●●●●●

Welcome back. How did you do? If you're like most people, you probably were able to recall the first few plays, one towards the end and possibly one or two of the plays in the middle that are the ones most frequently staged. It's unlikely that you were able to recall all fourteen plays in their exact order. However, if you did, shut the book now and try saying them in reverse order, or start at the eighth play and continue to the end. The point here is that after you learn the technique, you'll be able to say the names of the plays forward, backward, inside and out.

So what exactly is the link method and how do you use it? In its simplest form, the link method is an association of two pieces of information that can't be broken. The way that you make the association is by using your imagination and telling yourself a memorable story that connects the old information to the new information. Again, we know that our mind thinks in pictures; we have to be interested in the material we're trying to learn; we typically forget the mundane things in life but quickly remember information that's unusual or emotional; and we take in data through our senses. By using these facts, the process for the link method is to make up a simple story between the old and the new pieces of information. Using all of your senses to remember something new, you must actively associate the new information to the old information in some absurd, emotional, and unbelievable way. The stories you make up must be bursting with action or they'll be mundane. The images you create need to pique your interest, so the crazier the story is, the easier it will be remember it.

Since our mind thinks in pictures, the first step in remembering the list of Shakespeare's comedies is to turn the names of the plays into images. If you don't turn the plays into images, you'll be stuck trying to remember dry words and we don't think in words, we think in pictures. Remember the example of the elephant and the fireworks.

We'll now begin the Link Method. Below is a crazy story. Read it from start to finish without taking a break and as you read it, really try to picture all of the images. The more focused you are on seeing the story and making it come to life in your mind, the better your results will be.

One warm summer day, you find yourself walking through the woods. The sun is shining down through the trees. You feel the dried leaves crunch under your feet as you walk along the path. In the distance you see an old brick well with a bucket on a rope hanging above it. As you get closer to the well, you see that the letter "N" appears all over it. The letter "N" is written in bricks on the outside and the inside. The letter "N" is chiseled into the walls. You lean over and look into the well to see the bottom, but it's very dark and deep and cold. You yell "Hello, 'N' Well," and your voice echoes off the inside walls. *(The well described here is the*

13

*play **All's Well That Ends Well** turned into an image. The letter "N" will help you think of the word "Ends").*

As you lean over again to try to see the bottom of the well, your feet slip out from under you and you fall. The fall is long and you fear you'll hit the ground hard and you pray that when the fall ends that all will be well. Instead of crashing onto a brick bottom or splashing into a pool of water, you land on one thousand ice cream cones. You feel the cold ice cream mush all around you and you feel and hear the crunching of the sugar and wafer cones. You're not hurt at all and you love the feeling of the cold ice cream all around you. You pick up a large ice cream cone and see that it's your favorite flavor (maybe it's mint chocolate chip or maybe it's butter pecan or maybe it's just vanilla—you choose). You lick it and discover the taste is glorious. You relax and forget that you're at the bottom of the well. As you lick it, all your worries fade away, and as you lick it, you smile and enjoy the peace and quiet. (*The image you see in your mind "as you lick it" will trigger the play **As You Like It**).*

Suddenly, you hear screaming from the top of the well and when you look up, you see Robin Williams, Eddie Murphy, Steve Martin, Chris Rock, and Jerry Seinfeld. They're all staring down at you from the top of the well. Instead of trying to help pull you up though, they're all doing their comedy routines, but they constantly make errors. Their jokes don't make sense. They mess up their punch lines. They're in complete disarray. You think to yourself that you've never seen comedy done so poorly before and you've never seen comedians make so many errors. (*The image of the comedians making mistakes will make you think of the play **The Comedy of Errors**).*

The comedians finally get their act together and throw down a rope. They line up as if they were in a tug-of-war contest and stand one behind the other: first Robin, then Eddie, then Steve, then Chris, and finally Jerry. You drop your ice cream cone, grab the rope with both hands, wrap it around your waist, and give it a tug to let them know you're ready to be lifted up. Suddenly, the comedians make another error and instead of pulling you up carefully, they yank the rope so hard that you literally go flying up the shaft of the well, past the carved letter N's, and go soaring out of the top of the well and over one hundred yards into the forest. You crash through the branches and land with a thud on the ground. As you gather yourself, you realize that you're lying on top of something that is moving. You jump to your feet and are amazed when you see what was underneath you. Standing before you is the cutest little red cartoon heart dressed in a business suit, holding a briefcase. You think that you must have hit your head pretty hard and that you're seeing things, but right there in front of you is this little heart salesman. He dusts himself off, looks up at you, and says, "Good day, sir. I am a little heart and I am on my way to work, but I

14

am lost. Can you help me find my way?" (*The image of the lost heart salesman will help you think of the play* **Love's Labour's Lost**).

You look down at the heart and say, "Sure, I'll try to help you find your way to work. What exactly do you sell?" The heart opens his briefcase and takes out a collapsible ruler, a measuring tape, a set of measuring cups, and a variety of scales. He says, "I'm the world's best salesman of measuring devices. I sell rulers and measuring tapes to measure length. I sell measuring cups to measure liquid and flour. I sell scales to measure the weight of small objects and I sell scales for people to stand on so they can measure their weight. Would you like to buy a measuring cup or any of my measuring devices?" You say, "Sure, may I please buy a thermometer to measure the temperature?" The little heart salesman takes your money and hands you a pocket thermometer. (*The image of all the measuring devices will help you think of the play* **Measure for Measure**).

Just as you're about to say, "Thank you," both you and the little cartoon heart salesman hear something in the distance galloping toward you. You look up and see an old merchant with crazy gray hair and tattered clothes riding on the back of a huge deer as if it were a horse. The deer makes you remember a delicious venison meal you ate the night before and you imagine just how tasty this deer's meat would be. You see the massive deer charging at you, you feel the ground beneath your feet tremble, and you hear the old merchant screaming, "Whoa!" as the deer skids to a stop in front of you and the little heart. (*The image of the old merchant on the deer should make you think of the play* **The Merchant of Venice**). The old merchant looks down at the little cartoon heart salesman and says, "Where have you been, son? We have an appointment at Windsor Castle with all of the wives of the royal family." The merchant looks at you and says, "What are you both waiting for? Hop on." So you pick up the little heart, leap onto the massive deer, and hold onto the dusty old merchant's back.

The deer takes off galloping through the woods, leaping over fallen branches and dodging trees around every turn. The merchant pulls up on the reins once again and yells, "Whoa!" The deer comes to a stop and you realize that you're now in England, just outside Windsor Castle. You look into the massive window on the first floor and see there is a party taking place inside. The merchant guides the deer a little closer to help you get a better look. Inside, all of the wives of the royal family are dressed up as Mrs. Claus. They're having some sort of a Christmas party in the summer and you're completely intrigued. The wives are all walking around in Christmas costumes and you see them curtsying and saying, "Merry Christmas. Merry Christmas." You realize that they're rehearsing for a play that all of the Windsor wives put on for Christmas. (*The image of the*

*Windsor wives all saying "Merry Christmas" should make you think of the play **The Merry Wives of Windsor**).*

Suddenly, the deer bucks and kicks and you go flying off backward. As you tumble high in the sky, you see the little red cartoon heart salesman and the old merchant ride off in the distance. You finally come crashing down and land face-first in the sand. Your head is foggy and you feel like you're in a dream. You slowly push yourself up from the ground, your head spinning. Everything around you is in slow motion and you know you must be dreaming. You spit the sand from your mouth and brush the dirt away from your eyes. It's dark outside now and you look down at your watch, which says it's midnight. Even though it's midnight, your see that the beach where you landed is hopping with activity. There looks to be a beach soccer game taking place. People are playing everywhere. There are circus acts going on. You see leprechauns riding unicorns and you know you must be dreaming, but it's such a great dream that you don't want to wake up. It's the most enjoyable summer night that you ever remember experiencing. (*The images you see when you think about being in a dream state at midnight on the beach during summer should make you think of the play **A Midsummer Night's Dream**).*

You continue walking down the beach toward the soccer match and see it's a game between the England national team and the United States national team. The only player sitting on the U.S. bench is Freddy Adu. You walk up to Freddy Adu and see that he's just sitting there, doing absolutely nothing. You say, "Freddy Adu, what are you doing?" and he looks at you and screams back, "What does it look like I'm doing? I'm doing nothing. Freddy Adu is doing nothing. I should be playing out there right now, but no, Freddy Adu is doing nothing!" (*The image of Freddy Adu doing nothing and screaming at you that he's doing nothing should make you think of the play **Much Ado About Nothing**).*

Suddenly, your attention gets pulled to the right as you hear a loud crack of a whip. You jump up and run over to see what's going on. You realize that there's a lion tamer show taking place on the beach as part of the circus acts. The lion tamer has a huge whip in his right hand that he's cracking. In his left hand is a wooden chair. He's skilled at twirling his whip around and around above his head and then snapping it at the lion. But then you realize it's not a lion at all. It's a woman with a massive amount of red hair that looks like a lion's mane. She's kicking and shouting and acting insane. She's a total shrew. As she charges the lion tamer, she screams at him that he's an evil man who's oppressing women worldwide. He spins his whip above his head in circles and cracks it down toward the shrew as she lunges at him. (*The image of the lion tamer taming the shrew of a woman should make you think of the play **The Taming of the Shrew**).*

The lion tamer raises his right hand above his head and spins his whip around and around with incredible velocity. The whip is going so fast it looks like helicopter blades and the wind that it creates makes the sand around the lion tamer and the shrew rise off the beach and swirl. Suddenly, you feel the wind pick up and the sand starts to spin violently. The sand rises further and becomes a tornado cone spinning out of control. The weather instantly turns cold and the sky grows dark and ominous. A massive tempest of a storm rages and the sand tornado picks up even more speed. Rain pours down as lightning shoots from the black clouds. The tempest rages out of control, causing beach chairs and people to fly through the air. As the temperature plummets even more, it begins to snow and sleet and hail. You take out your pocket thermometer that you purchased from the little cartoon heart salesman and you see that the temperature is now minus fifteen degrees. You shiver and look for shelter, but the tempest has consumed the beach and you can't find safety anywhere. (*The images of the tempest/storm and the thermometer used to take the temperature should help you think of the play* **The Tempest**).

Suddenly, you feel the ground tremble like it did when the old merchant on the big deer came galloping toward you in the forest, but this time the ground rumbles much harder. You cover your eyes to protect them from the debris flying around from the tempest. You peek through your fingers and see what looks like a dozen horses galloping toward you. As the horses approach, you see that there are knights in full armor on each horse. The knights have arrived to save everyone from the tempest. Eleven knights pass right by you and grab people off the sand and pull them onto their horses. Finally, the twelfth knight at the back reaches down just as he gets to you, yanks you up by your shirt, and throws you on the back of his horse. You wrap your arms around the cold steel of his armor. Your face is pressed against the knight's back and you finally feel safe. (*The images of the twelfth knight saving you should help you think of the play* **Twelfth Night**).

The horse gallops for a very long time, leaping through the snow that the crazy tempest dumped all over the land. Everywhere you look is pure white. After what feels like days of riding, you hear the knight say, "Whoa!" and the horse slows down to a walking pace. You look around and see you're now in Italy. The other eleven knights on their horses are slowly walking in front of you down the main road of the town. You see thousands of people lined up on both sides of the road holding banners and signs that read *Verona Welcomes the Twelve Knights*. Even though there's snow everywhere and it's bitter cold, people are lining the streets and cheering as the knights ride through town. At the end of the road is a castle made of ornately carved granite. The twelve horses come to a stop in front of the castle, and two Italian businessmen wearing fine Italian suits help each

17

knight and their passenger off the horses. The two gentlemen of Verona, Italy that approach you and your knight move with grace and sophistication. They present themselves with confidence and with the utmost respect, gently extending a hand to help you down from the horse. Once you're safely on the ground, the two gentlemen say in unison, "On behalf of the entire country of Italy, we humbly welcome you to our beautiful city of Verona." (*The images of the two Italian businessmen saying "Welcome to Verona" should help you think of the play **The Two Gentlemen of Verona**).*

As you and your knight walk up the pathway toward the castle, you see beautifully created snowmen, snow-animals, and snow-buildings on either side. You're amazed at the fine detail of the work that went into creating the snow structures. They seem lifelike. At the gate just before the doors to the castle there are two giant snow-cats perched on their hind legs. The structures make you think of the concrete lions people have on their driveways, but these snow-cats are giant in size and very realistic. Then you realize that the tails of the snow-cats are waving back and forth, brushing away the snow from the pathway. The snow that the tails are wiping swirl around in the sky and gently fall back down to the ground. It looks and feels like you're inside a beautiful snow globe that was just shaken. The fluffy, powdery snow falls gently around you. The tails of the snow-cats slowly come to a stop and you see the pathway to the castle has been wiped clean. (*The images of the snow-cats' tails brushing the snow off the ground and making it fall all around you should help you think of the play **The Winter's Tale**).*

The knight motions for you to enter the castle, and as you approach the door, you hear music playing and realize there's a party taking place in your honor. You go inside and see the most amazing extravaganza you've ever witnessed in your life. Standing around the well with the letter "N" all over it, licking ice cream cones and messing up their jokes, are Robin Williams, Eddie Murphy, Steve Martin, Chris Rock, and Jerry Seinfeld. You look to the right and see the little cartoon heart in a suit selling his measuring devices to the old merchant on his deer and to all of the wives from Windsor Castle who are dressed in their Mrs. Claus costumes while they say, "Merry Christmas." To the left you see a dreamland night-time themed beach party where Freddy Adu is standing on the side doing nothing as he watches the shrew tamer crack his whip at the crazy woman. The music thumps louder and louder and people start raving. Everyone is throwing things all over the place. There are napkins and cups and plates and food flying and swirling all around the room and it feels like you're in the middle of a massive storm. Then the crowd in the middle of the room opens to reveal the twelve knights in a break dance battle versus the two gentlemen from Verona and the snow-cats who are spinning on their tails. You take a deep breath, laugh, and join in the dance battle.

Please take a break for a few minutes right now. Get up and walk away from this book. Let the silly story that you just read simply be and don't put any pressure on yourself to recall anything just yet. If you really saw the images in your imagination as you read the story, then your recollection will be fine. Go on and take a quick five minute break now.

●●●●●●●●

Welcome back. Now we'll test your memory to see how well you were able to apply the Link and Chain method to help you remember Shakespeare's comedies. The important point here is that as you're first learning this method, you shouldn't rush to say the thing you're trying to recall—the name of the play in this case—but rather take your time to retell yourself the story in detail because it's through the associations and the stories that the information will come back to you. When you get stuck and can't remember something, it means that your story wasn't powerful enough or you rushed past a certain part in retelling yourself the story. If you take time to recall the finer details of your story, the information you're trying to remember will come back to you.

Let's start at the beginning of the story. You were walking in the forest and came upon the well with the letter "N" all over it. Think about all the details of the well and you'll eventually remember that the well described here is the play *All's Well That Ends Well* turned into an image and that the letter "N" helps you think of the word "Ends." Then you fell into the well and landed on all the ice cream cones. Really remember how it felt and how the ice cream cones tasted as you licked them. You'll then quickly remember that the image you see in your mind "as you lick it" triggers the play *As You Like It.*

What happened next? In your mind, look up the shaft of the well and what do you hear and see? Really retell yourself the story. Do you see all the comedians making mistakes as they try to deliver their comedy routines? Which comedians to you see? Soon the image of the comedians making mistakes will help you think of the play *The Comedy of Errors.*

What's next? Do you climb out of the well alone? How do you get out of the well? Remember the rope being sent down by the comedians? Do they lift you out gently or do they yank you up? Where do you go soaring when you get pulled out of the well? Do you land on a soft bed? No. You landed in the forest. What did the ground feel like? Did you land on something? Yes, you did. What's moving underneath you? It's the cartoon heart in a suit, right? He's lost on his way to work. How cute was the little cartoon heart? This image of the lost heart salesman will help you think of the play *Love's Labour's Lost.*

What does the heart salesman sell? Really see all of his products as he pulls them out to show you. Do you see measuring cups and rulers and scales? The images of all the measuring devices will help you think of the play *Measure for Measure.*

Then the ground starts to rumble and what do you see coming toward you? Is it a horse? No? Then what is it? Really see the old merchant riding on the back of the deer. What does he look like? What is he wearing? How big is the deer? Do you think about a steak? No, you should be thinking about a venison dinner. The image of the old merchant on the deer should make you think of the play *The Merchant of Venice.*

Then what happens? Does the merchant ride off on the deer alone or do you and the cartoon heart get onto the deer and ride off with him? Correct. You got on the back of the deer and galloped off on a long ride. Where did you end up? Are you in New York City? No. You ended up in Windsor, England outside Windsor Castle. What was going on inside the castle? Did you see a costume party? Who was at the party? What were they doing and saying? Really remember looking through the window. The image of the Windsor wives all dressed up in costume and saying "Merry Christmas" should make you think of the play *The Merry Wives of Windsor.*

Do you dismount and walk off into the sunset? No. Remember that the deer bucks and what happens next. Do you remember going flying off backward and soaring through the air? If not, it's because you didn't make the image vividly clear in your mind as you were reading the story. It's critical for this technique to work that you use your creative instincts as an actor and really let your imagination run wild. Truly see all the bright colors and details of the events unfolding before your mind's eye. Truly experience all the emotions, smell all the scents, feel all the surfaces, taste all the wonderful tastes.

Getting back to the story, you should now be flying through the air and landing face-first on the beach. You knocked your head pretty bad, and as you get up and walk around a bit woozy, what do you see happening on the beach at night? The images of you being in a dream state at midnight on the beach during summer should make you think of the play *A Midsummer Night's Dream.*

Then there's the beach soccer match, but between which two countries? Do you see a U.S. player sitting and doing nothing? Who is the player? Is it Landon Donavon? No, it's Freddy Adu. What's he doing? The image of Freddy Adu doing nothing and screaming at you that he's doing nothing should make you think of the play *Much Ado About Nothing.*

What happens next? What do you hear? Do you remember the crack of the whip? Do you see the lion tamer? What is he wearing? Is he cracking his whip at a lion or something else? It's the crazy woman, right? What do you see her doing? How is she acting? The image of the lion tamer taming the shrew of a woman should make you think of the play *The Taming of the Shrew.*

Then the lion tamer spins his whip around fast above his head and what happens? Do you feel the weather change? Does it get hot or does it get cold and rain violently? What happens to the sand on the beach? Do you remember taking out the thermometer that you bought from the cartoon heart salesman to see what the temperature was? Does it feel like a massive storm is blowing all around you? The images of the tempest/storm and the thermometer used to take the temperature should help you think of the play ***The Tempest.***

Do you die on the beach in the storm or are you rescued? Who saves you? What do you see? Does a boat come to rescue you or is it twelve knights on horseback? How does it feel when your knight picks you up and you ride off holding onto his cold armor? The images of the twelfth knight saving you should help you think of the play ***Twelfth Night.***

What happens next? Where do you and your knight ride to? Do you go back to the forest or to the Windsor Castle? No, you end up in Italy. But where in Italy are you? Are you in Rome? No, you're in Verona and what's going on as you ride down the road? Are people there to see and greet you? Is there a parade and banners? What's going on with the weather? Is it hot or is the entire land covered in snow? How do you get off the horse? Who helps you down? Do you remember the gentlemen dressed in fine Italian suits? The images of the two Italian businessmen saying "Welcome to Verona" should help you think of the play ***The Two Gentlemen of Verona.***

After you come down from the horse, where do you go? Do you walk into town to go shopping? No, you walk toward the castle. And what lines the sides of the path to the castle? Do you remember all of the snowmen, snow-animals, and snow-buildings? What happens when you see the tails of the snow-cats? Do you see the tails moving around brushing the snow out of the way to clear a path for you? Do you feel the snow falling down around you like you're in a snow globe? The images of the snow-cats' tails brushing the snow off the ground and making it fall all around you should help you think of the play ***The Winter's Tale.***

Then the knight motions for you to enter the castle, and as you approach the door, you hear music playing and realize there's a party taking place in your honor. You go inside and see the most amazing extravaganza you've ever witnessed in your life. Standing around the well with the letter "N" all over it, licking ice cream cones and messing up their jokes, are Robin Williams, Eddie Murphy, Steve Martin, Chris Rock, and Jerry Seinfeld. You look to the right and see the little cartoon heart in a suit selling his measuring devices to the old merchant on his deer and to all of the wives from the Windsor Castle who are dressed in their Mrs. Claus costumes while they say "Merry Christmas." To the left you see a dreamland nighttime-themed beach party where Freddy Adu is standing on the side doing nothing as he watches the shrew tamer crack his whip at the crazy woman. The music thumps louder and louder and people start raving. Everyone is throwing things all over the place. There are napkins and cups and plates and food flying and swirling all around the room and it feels like you're in the middle of a massive storm. Then the crowd in the middle of the room opens to reveal the twelve knights in a break dance battle versus the two gentlemen from Verona and the snow-cats who are spinning on their tails. You take a deep breath, laugh, and join in the dance battle.

This brings us back to the beginning or the end depending upon how you look at it. In either case, you now have vivid images as told through a memorable story to help you remember Shakespeare's comedies. Before we go further, let's see how well you can remember Shakespeare's comedies on your own. Without looking back to the previous pages or forward to what's coming next, fill in the lines below.

## Shakespeare's Comedies

- _____
- _____
- _____
- _____
- _____
- _____
- _____
- _____
- _____
- _____
- _____
- _____
- _____
- _____

Here is the list again so you can see how well you did.

# Shakespeare's Comedies

- All's Well That Ends Well
- As You Like It
- The Comedy of Errors
- Love's Labour's Lost
- Measure for Measure
- The Merchant of Venice
- The Merry Wives of Windsor
- A Midsummer Night's Dream
- Much Ado About Nothing
- The Taming of the Shrew
- The Tempest
- Twelfth Night
- Two Gentlemen of Verona
- The Winter's Tale

You may wonder how we move from remembering lists to remembering your monologues or dialogues. Right now, we're building your skills with the technique of linking and associating. In the upcoming chapter, we'll explore Peg Lists to further expand your memory skills. Shortly after that, we'll apply the technique to sample lines. It's important to crawl before you walk, walk before you run, run before you sprint, and sprint before you soar.

So what happens if the information that you're trying to remember doesn't interest you? How do you go from not caring about the information and constantly forgetting it to recalling it instantly? Your interest level in the material being memorized plays an important role in how easily the information is memorized. So if you're not interested in the material, you have to manufacture interest to get the memorization ball rolling. That means that when you create the association stories, they must be crazy and wildly entertaining so that you actually like them. Making the stories bizarre and outrageous will help you be interested in the words you're trying to remember.

So how do you do that? How do you make a story bizarre and outrageous? The answer depends on what kind of a person you are. If you're a gentle person who sees the world full of fluffy white bunny rabbits, then you might consider making your stories violent in nature. By going to the polar opposite of who you are at the core, you automatically make what you're trying to remember not mundane to you. The more opposite from your nature you can get your stories to be, the easier it will be to remember them.

The other approach is to simply go overboard within your nature. Again, if you're a gentle person and everything is sunshine and rainbows, if you make your stories totally over-the-top happy, you'll be on the path to euphoria in your world, and that is certainly not mundane. My suggestion is to try both approaches and whichever one helps you remember the information better, that's the one you should stick with.

Remember that all of this is happening inside your mind. It's all within your imagination and no one ever needs to know what you're doing or how you're remembering things. Frankly, it's no one's business how you get to the information, ever. That's private, and I suggest never sharing it with others, because it will be bizarre to them if they don't know the techniques and they'll likely judge you. That judgment will make you question yourself and the technique and the last thing you want to do is to stifle your creative instincts as an actor.

Also, recall that people have different ways to absorb information. We take in data through our senses. We see things, we hear things, we taste things, we smell things, and we feel things. So the more details you can add into your stories that link back to as many senses as possible, especially the ones that you're drawn to, the more interest you'll have in the information you're trying to remember. The more interest you have, the faster you'll recall the information. Rest assured that we'll soon stop using the word "information" and will replace it with words like "your monologue" and "your dialogue."

It's time to take another break. Remember that the more breaks you take, the more starts and stops you'll have, and the more starts and stops you have, the more you'll remember. So walk away for a while. Do something completely unrelated to memorization techniques. Go outside. Exercise. Grab a bite to eat. Whatever you do, though, don't continue reading right now. Whether you feel like you need a break or not, your brain has just absorbed a lot of information and you need to process it.

●●●●●●●●

# PEG LISTS

Welcome back. Before we explore the next system known as Peg Lists or File/Folder Systems, let's see if you can say all fourteen of Shakespeare's comedies. Don't cheat by looking back. Make sure to go slowly and retell yourself the story in vivid detail. Let the silly and bizarre images pop into your mind without judgment and you'll quickly be able to name them all.

## Shakespeare's Comedies

- _____
- _____
- _____
- _____
- _____
- _____
- _____
- _____
- _____
- _____
- _____
- _____
- _____
- _____

How did you do? If you missed any, it was because the story wasn't memorable for you. That's actually a good thing when that happens as you begin learning this technique because it exposes parts of the associations that didn't work. You can then go back to that specific section and expand or replace the story to make it more meaningful, interesting, bizarre, and memorable for your style of thinking.

It's now time to move on to the Peg Lists. Imagine for a moment that you go to an audition and when you get there, there's a row of wooden pegs in the wall for everyone to hang up their jackets. Picture yourself hanging your coat onto that wooden peg and then walking into the audition room. Assume that nobody steals your jacket and assume that the wooden peg in the wall does not break, regardless of how long you're away, when you come back from your audition (which I know you nailed), your coat will still be there.

A similar analogy is a metal filing cabinet filled with folders. Imagine that you open the top drawer and pull out a folder that says "Headshots," and you pull out another folder that says "Résumés." Inside the Headshots folder, you place fifty of your new 8x10 pictures and inside the Résumés folder you place fifty copies of your updated résumé. Pretend that you receive a call from your agent to go on an audition and you're told to bring your latest headshot and résumé. Without question, you know that when you open the filing cabinet and pull out the Headshots and Résumés folders that your new headshot and résumé will be there. They will always be there until you take them out and either use them, replace them, or throw them away.

Well, the Peg List system is a mental process of creating pegs or folders that will always be there no matter what happens. After you associate new information to the peg or file, when you think of the old thing that you already know (the peg or file), the new information you're trying to recall will be there as well. This probably seems a bit abstract right now, but once you work through the process, it will be perfectly clear. Also note that anything can be turned into a peg list—numbers, locations, objects, body parts, your house, and so on.

# THE NUMBER PEG LISTS

For the purposes of the next few sections, we'll focus on three different number peg lists: the Number-Rhyme Peg List, the Number-Association Peg List, and the Number-Shape Peg List. Below is a chart with suggestions for these three number peg lists. Ultimately, the memory technique works best when you create your own peg lists, but the suggestions below will help you get started.

| NUMBER | RHYME | ASSOCIATION | SHAPE |
|--------|-------|-------------|-------|
| 1 | Sun (Bun, Gun) | Unicycle | Candle |
| 2 | Shoe (Glue, Zoo) | Bicycle | Swan |
| 3 | Tree (Bee, Tea) | Tricycle | Heart |
| 4 | Door (Boar, Shore) | Car | Sail |
| 5 | Hive (Dive, Drive) | Glove | Fish Hook |
| 6 | Sticks (Bricks, Tricks) | Six-pack of Soda | Elephant's Trunk |
| 7 | Heaven | Pair of Dice | Boomerang |
| 8 | Gate (Bait, Crate) | Roller Skates | Snowman |
| 9 | Wine (Sign, Vine) | Cat | Balloon on a String |
| 10 | Hen (Men, Pen) | Bowling | Bat and Ball |

# THE NUMBER-RHYME PEG LIST

In the Number-Rhyme Peg List, you'll create an image as the peg that you'll always go back to and associate new information to. This image will rhyme with a number. In the matrix below, the word sun rhymes with the number one, so the image of the sun is your Number-Rhyme peg for the number one. The word shoe rhymes with the number two, so the image of a shoe is your Number-Rhyme peg for the number two. The word tree rhymes with the number three, so the image of a tree is your Number-Rhyme peg for the number three. The word door rhymes with the number four, so the image of a door is your Number-Rhyme peg for the number four. The word hive rhymes with the number five, so the image of a hive is your Number-Rhyme peg for the number five. The word sticks rhymes with the number six, so the image of sticks is your Number-Rhyme peg for the number six. The word heaven rhymes with the number seven, so the image of heaven is your Number-Rhyme peg for the number seven. The word gate rhymes with the number eight, so the image of a gate is your Number-Rhyme peg for the number eight. The word wine rhymes with the number nine, so the image of a bottle of wine is your Number-Rhyme peg for the number nine. Finally, the word hen rhymes with the number ten, so the image of a hen is your Number-Rhyme peg for the number ten.

Below is a list of ten silly things for you to remember. The new information that you'll be "pegging" to your Number-Rhyme Peg List is a Hairy Clergyman, Crawfish Shells, Straws made from Leaves, Steel Adding Machine, Sand in my Eyes, Clifford the Big Red Dog, An Eel playing a Kazoo, Corn on the Cob, Garfield the Cat on the John, and Gordon Ramsay with a Microphone.

| NUMBER | RHYME | REMEMBER THIS LIST |
|--------|-------|--------------------|
| 1 | Sun | Hairy Clergyman |
| 2 | Shoe | Crawfish Shells |
| 3 | Tree | Straws made from Leaves |
| 4 | Door | Steel Adding Machine |
| 5 | Hive | Sand in my Eyes |
| 6 | Sticks | Clifford the Big Red Dog |
| 7 | Heaven | An Eel playing a Kazoo |
| 8 | Gate | Corn on the Cob |
| 9 | Wine | Garfield the Cat on the John |
| 10 | Hen | Gordon Ramsay with a Microphone |

Let's start with number one. Your Number-Rhyme peg for the number one is the sun and the thing you're trying to remember is a hairy clergyman. Can you imagine that you're at church, sitting in the middle of a packed congregation? The sun is beating down strongly and the temperature is sweltering. You see people sweating and fanning themselves. The sunlight is pouring through the beautifully colored stain glass windows and streaks of red, blue, orange, and purple are reflected from behind the pastor across the church to the back wall. The clergyman is on the pulpit preaching an amazing sermon about forgiveness. He's inspiring and the entire congregation is visibly moved by his words. He stands behind the podium with a bible in his right hand. He's a tall man with long, thick, dark black hair and a full dark beard. As you see him hold up the bible, you notice that his arm hair is poking out from under his sleeve. He is equally as hot as the congregation from the scorching sun and you see sweat dripping from his forehead through his beard and onto the podium before him.

Suddenly, the sun gets significantly hotter and brighter. The colors from the stained glass windows glow with increased intensity. The windows melt and molten glass drips onto the church floor. You feel the wooden seat under you heat up and everyone in the church panics. The clergyman raises his voice to calm the congregation, but suddenly a burning ray of sunlight hits his dark beard and catches it on fire. The flames quickly engulf the thick black hair on his head. Then his arm hair catches fire. You rush up to the pulpit and grab the hairy clergyman, pull him to the ground, and roll him back and forth to put out the flames. You grab a pitcher of water and pour it on the hairy clergyman. As the flames go out, you hear the sound of his beard and hair crinkling and cracking into pieces. You sit him up and realize he's fine. You got to him in time and no real damage was done. The room, however, is full of burning sunlight and the wooden pews suddenly catch on fire. The clergyman stands up, and despite having his beard and hair mostly burned away, he quickly orders everyone out of the church and onto the front lawn. The entire congregation streams out of the church just as the fire trucks arrive. Everyone is safe. No one is seriously hurt, but the hairy clergyman is missing most of his hair and half of his beard. Everyone walks away safely as the firefighters and paramedics tend to the hairy clergyman.

In this association story, we've vividly pegged the hairy clergyman to the sun. So when you go back to the thing that will always be there, the Number-Rhyme peg of the sun for the number one, you'll imagine the sun first, but then you'll ask yourself: What is the sun doing? What is being affected by the sun? What is interacting with the sun? And you'll easily retell yourself the story of the sun burning in the church and the hairy clergyman catching on fire.

Let's move on to number two. Your Number-Rhyme peg for the number two is a shoe and the thing you're trying to remember is crawfish shells. We must now peg the image of crawfish shells to a shoe in some crazy way that will interest you, not be mundane, and be as memorable as possible. When people first use this system, they tend to not allow their imagination to go as far as it should. Meaning, it's natural to simply imagine there are crawfish shells in your shoes and when you put them on you feel the shells on your feet. That's mildly interesting, but definitely not powerful enough to be memorable. Remember that in order to remember something new, you have to associate it with something you already know in some strange, bizarre, crazy, insane, funny, silly, or amazing way. Just putting crawfish shells into your shoes does not reach that goal.

So let's allow our imaginations to run wild. Imagine that you're in a crawfish eating contest in New Orleans. Picture yourself seated at a long table up on the main stage in front of thousands of screaming fans. ESPN is airing this crawfish eating contest, and you're seated next to last year's champion. (It's time for you to imagine what that person looks like. Describe them in detail to yourself). The rules of the contest are as follows: Run from the table to the crawfish tank and use your shoes to scoop out as many crawfish as possible. Run back to the table, pour all the crawfish from your shoes onto the table, eat the crawfish, shove the shells in your shoes, put your shoes on, crush the shells as you run to your shell-dumping bucket, take your shoes off, dump out the shells, and repeat the process for ten minutes. The winner is the person who has the most crawfish shells in their bucket when time expires.

The announcer says, "Ready, set, go!" and you, along with last year's champion and the other eight contestants, all run over to the crawfish tank. You take your shoes off, scoop out as many crawfish as you can fit in your shoes, and run back to the table. You're the fourth person back so you know you have to pick up the pace. With the crawfish on the table in front of you, you rip them apart, shove the food into your mouth, and stuff the shells back into your shoes. You eat fifty-five crawfish in total and have all fifty-five shells inside your shoes. You jam your feet into your shoes, being very careful to not let any crawfish shells fall out. You feel the sharp edges on the bottom of your feet and you feel the shells squish between your toes. You feel one sharp crawfish shell poke your arch and you feel a sting as it pierces your skin. You hobble over to your dumping bucket and remove your shoes. You pour the crushed crawfish shells into your bucket, turn, and sprint back to the crawfish tank to get your second round.

You repeat the process and make it back to the table with sixty-four more crawfish. You rip and eat and stuff the shells into your shoes again and again. After you eat all sixty-four crawfish, you jam your feet into your shoes and run to your dumping bucket. You're slipping out of your shoes and see a few crawfish shells poking out the side, so you push them back in and slow down just a bit. You dump your second load of crawfish shells from your shoes into your bucket, making sure to bang out all of the shells again. You look down and see crawfish shells actually on all your toes like a little puppet show. You use your shoe to wipe them off your toes and into the bucket. You turn around again and race to the tank for a third time. The announcer calls out, "One minute left!" You pick up the pace, fill your shoes to the very top with crawfish, and when you get back to the table you dump out eighty-two more crawfish.

You take a deep breath and begin shredding through the crustaceans, biting and ripping and stuffing the shells into your shoes. You look at the clock and see it counting down from twenty seconds. You eat your last five crawfish, stuff the shells into your shoes, and push your wet, slippery, cut-up feet into your shoes. You feel the sting of the crawfish shells against your cut soles, but you run as fast as you can to the dumping bucket. You pour out all of the crawfish shells from your shoes and bang them together to make sure every last one is out just as the buzzer sounds.

The contest is over and you look at the buckets of the other contestants. Only one bucket has crawfish shells as high as yours and it's the bucket of last year's champion. The ESPN announcer waits to be handed the official ruling and you put your shoes back on while you wait. The announcer brings the microphone to his mouth and says, "We have a new champion this year!" You scream and kick off your shoes as he announces your name.

Now when you think about your Number-Rhyme peg image of the shoe, you'll see the insane story of the crawfish eating contest and all the crawfish shells inside your shoes. Think back for a moment about the sun. What images come to mind? Do you see the hot sun burning through the window at the church and do you eventually see the hairy clergyman catching on fire? I'm sure you do.

It's time for number three. Your Number-Rhyme peg for the number three is a tree and the thing you're trying to remember is straws made from leaves. We must now create an association between a tree and straws made from leaves. Again, a simple but ineffective story would be to pick a leaf off the tree and roll it into a straw. That's boring, mundane, and contains nothing memorable to manufacture any interest. Use your acting skills here and exercise that imagination. What could you possibly be doing with a leaf to make it into a straw and how does that tie back to the tree?

Just in case you're wondering why you have to memorize this list of ten seemingly unrelated and silly things, please remember to not judge yourself or the technique. Just judge the results at the end. Everything presented in this book has a very specific purpose of building a common set of vocabulary upon which we'll build and master a variety of memorization techniques, and ultimately you'll have the power to remember your lines. But again, you have to first learn and then master the system before you jump to delivering that perfect monologue. Getting back to the tree, the leaves, and the straws, what images come to your mind? Here's a suggestion, but if you have something that works better for you, without question, you should use what you create. The more you use the stories created with your own imagination and your own spin, the faster you'll master this technique.

Picture yourself walking through a meadow and ahead in the distance you hear someone sobbing. It's a deep cry and they sound like they're in a lot of pain. You rush toward the sound, but as the sound gets louder you don't see anyone around. The only thing close to the crying sound is a very old and brittle tree that looks like it's moments away from dying and falling over. Suddenly, you realize that the crying is coming from the tree itself. You approach the tree slowly and you hear it weeping. It's lost nearly all of its leaves. You touch the tree trunk and feel its shallow breathing. You ask the tree, "What can I do to help you?" and the tree replies softly, "Water." You look to your left and see one of those old water pumps with a rusted metal handle. You run to the water pump and move the lever up and down, so that water flows out of the pump and down the channel. The water quickly fills the bucket on the ground.

You grab the bucket and rush back over to the dying tree and hold the bucket out in front of you. The tree sees the water, and then something amazing happens. The branches with the last few leaves on them all bend toward the bucket. As the branches approach the water, the leaves curl into long straws. The tree dips each branch and the straws made from leaves into the bucket and sips the water through the leaf-straws. You hear gulping noises as the water is sucked through the straws made from the leaves and suddenly the tree begins to rejuvenate. The water has replenished its essence. The tree stands upright. The branches grow stronger. Hundreds of leaves instantly form on the branches and within moments the tree is standing proud and full of life and color.

The straws made from leaves suck the last bit of water from the bucket and then the branches withdraw themselves and the straws unroll and spread out wide. The tree takes a deep breath and says, "Thank you." You run over and fill the bucket one last time and leave it at the base of the trunk. You walk away in amazement of the wonders of nature.

Now when you think of your Number-Rhyme peg for the number three, you'll see the tree and you'll visualize the tree using its leaves as straws to drink the water from the bucket.

Your Number-Rhyme peg for the number four is a door and the thing you're trying to remember is a steel adding machine. We must now create an association between a door and a steel adding machine. It's important that you first create a strong image for the door. It's not just a simple wooden door with no unique attributes. Rather, this door should be distinctive with memorable characteristics. Let's imagine that you're at the bank and you need to make a withdrawal. You approach the counter and tell the clerk that you would like access to the vault to get into your safety deposit box. The manager brings you into a secure room where the vault is. Before you stands the massive steel door of the vault, but instead of a dial combination and a multi-handled spinning wheel, sticking out of the center of the metal door is a vintage steel adding machine in pristine condition. Even though it appears to be built in the early 1900s, the adding machine looks brand new. The manager tells you that in order to open the massive vault door, you must enter your secret combination of numbers into the steel adding machine. You walk to the door and touch the cold metal. The door stands twelve feet high and twelve feet wide. By the size of the four steel hinges on the left side, you imagine the vault door is at least three feet thick. The steel adding machine has been professionally installed in the center of the door. As you run your fingers along the edge where the steel adding machine meets the metal door, you can't feel any seams. It's as if the steel adding machine has organically grown out from the center of the metal door like a pregnant woman's belly.

As you look closer at the steel adding machine, you see that each number is a one-foot circle made from brushed black steel and the number itself is an inlay of silver. You enter your twelve-digit code, knowing that after you press down each number you'll have to use two hands and all your weight to pull down the massive steel handle on the right side of the adding machine in order to register your entry. The first set of four numbers is the year you were born. The second set of four numbers is the year your mother was born and the third set of four numbers is the year your father was born. You press down the first number and are surprised at how smoothly the steel circle moves down. After you feel the number stop moving, you hear a loud click acknowledging that the number has been fully depressed. The weight of the return mechanism pushing the number back up to its original position throws you back slightly and you stumble, but quickly regain your balance. You step to the right and reach up with both hands to grab hold of the long steel arm. It reminds you of a massive slot machine in Las Vegas. You jump a few inches off the ground to get as much torque as possible to help you pull the lever down. As the arm moves down, your feet steady themselves and you yank the steel arm harder. It swings past your head and down toward your hips and you use your full body weight to push it down until it clicks into position. Suddenly, the arm springs back up, moving to its upright position. You hang on for the ride and end up about one foot off the ground. You let go of the lever and drop back down to the floor.

One number complete, eleven more to go. You repeat the process eleven more times and once the lever reaches its upright position for the last time, the steel adding machine rotates forward. It looks like it's doing a somersault, and on the back side of the steel adding machine is the multi-arm spinning wheel that you first expected to see. You grab hold of the spinning wheel and spin it like you're steering a yacht into harbor. You hear a loud click and hiss as if an eighteen-wheel truck just released its air pressure. The massive steel door pops open slightly on the right side and you grab hold of the spinning wheel, set your feet, and pull the heavy door toward you. As you open the vault and walk inside past the door, you see the steel adding machine now sitting on the inside of the door. The manager says that he will now close the door behind you and to exit you'll need to repeat the twelve-number process from the inside. The massive door slowly closes and you hear it lock into place. You take a deep breath and walk to your safety deposit box as you rub your sore hands.

What images do you see now when you think about your peg for the number four? Do you see a simple door or do you see something with much more detail? Can you quickly move from recalling your door peg of the massive vault door to the steel adding machine? What do you think of when you read crawfish shells? Do you think about a shoe? Do you think about the crawfish eating contest? What comes to mind when you read the word sun? Do you feel the heat of the church as the sun pours through the stained glass windows? Do you see the hairy clergyman catching on fire?

Little by little, the technique of pegging new information to your peg list will become second nature. Have fun with it. Use your creative imagination to make the stories memorable. Fill them with as many details, action, and emotion as possible. Manufacture interest by making the story and association as wonderful and bizarre as you possibly can.

Your Number-Rhyme peg for the number five is a hive, like a beehive, and the thing you're trying to remember is sand in my eyes. We must now create an association between a beehive and sand in my eyes. As before, the stranger you make the story, the faster you'll manufacture the interest needed to help you recall the new information.

Let's imagine that you're walking through a nice meadow. It's springtime, the flowers are in bloom, and the sun is blowing gently through the trees. It's a beautiful day. You come across a tree that seems to be buzzing and you stop to look up. You see something you've never seen before. It's a beehive hanging from one of the lower branches, and it appears to be glowing. It's about two feet wide and four feet high, which is the largest hive you've ever seen in person or in a picture. It's bright gold and appears to be illuminated from inside.

As you walk carefully toward the hive, the buzzing gets louder and you see something pouring out of the hole at the bottom. You were expecting to see honey dripping out, but what's coming out of the bottom looks like sand. It confuses you, and you move a few steps closer. The buzzing gets even louder and the hive starts to sway back and forth from all

34

of the bees flying around it. You reach out your hand with an open palm facing upward and put it into the path of the falling sand. You instantly yank your hand back because the hot sand stings and burns. It makes no sense. Why would there be sand shooting out of the bottom of a beehive?

Suddenly, the hive tilts its hole toward you and starts to throb and glow more than before. Then, a fire hose-like stream of molten sand starts shooting out of the hive and hits you right in the face. The hot sand singes your eyes. You put your hands to your face to protect your eyes, but it's too late. The hot sticky sand has burrowed itself into your cornea, retina, and under your eyelids, and it burns with vicious pain. You run around in a panic screaming, "I've got sand in my eyes. I've got sand in my eyes. I've got sand in my eyes."

Sadly, this story doesn't end happily with you being saved by some magical creature. You're left with sand scars in your eyes from this terribly painful experience. Clearly, this would never happen. The point here is we don't want reality. We don't want logical stories because logic applied to these memory techniques keeps things in a box and stifles creativity. Even though in real life sand may never shoot from a beehive, for our purposes it does.

Take a ten minute break now. You've been reading for a while and should walk away again simply to leverage the natural way your mind works. Close the book now even if you want to keep reading. You'll thank me later when you look back at how much you've learned.

●●●●●●●●

Welcome back. I hope you gave yourself time to relax during your break. Let's see what you can recall so far. Fill in the blank sections of the grid below. To do this, don't rush right to the answer. Like before, take your time to retell yourself the story. As you recall the details of the story, the information you're trying to learn will come back very quickly. Make sure not to turn back or forward to peek at the answers on the other pages. Really challenge yourself to remember the information.

The objective here is to learn new skills to help you remember your lines, so by mastering the basics now, you'll be able to more quickly apply them in the upcoming sections where we'll explore monologues and dialogues. Just think how much more productive your rehearsals will be when you're off-book long before you ever were before. After you get past the line memorization requirement—often the most monotonous and uncreative part of the acting process—you can get deep into the aspects of acting that you love—the character development, the emotional and psychological breakdown of the script, and the development of the relationships with the other characters.

Until you have your lines down cold, you'll be restrained from making the progress needed to create a believable character who lives truthfully under the imaginary circumstances of the playwright. Look at the grid below and tell yourself the stories that you read before. Can you recall the list? Can you recall your pegs? Take time to remember the missing information now.

| NUMBER | RHYME | REMEMBER THIS LIST |
|--------|-------|--------------------|
| 1 | Sun | |
| 2 | | Crawfish Shells |
| 3 | Tree | |
| 4 | | Steel Adding Machine |
| 5 | Hive | |

●●●●●●●●

How did you do? Here is the list of information you should have easily remembered.

| NUMBER | RHYME | REMEMBER THIS LIST |
|--------|-------|--------------------|
| 1 | Sun | Hairy Clergyman |
| 2 | Shoe | Crawfish Shells |
| 3 | Tree | Straws made from Leaves |
| 4 | Door | Steel Adding Machine |
| 5 | Hive | Sand in my Eyes |

If you didn't remember some of the items, you must ask yourself why. The only answer is that the story wasn't meaningful enough to you. If the stories presented in this book didn't spark interest or you didn't relate to them, then it makes perfect sense that you'd have difficulty remembering the missing information. Again, in order to remember something new, it can't be mundane and you must have interest in it.

If you missed any of the items above, go back now and make up your own stories. The sooner you create the associations from your own imagination, the stronger your connection to the information will be and the faster you'll recall the thing you're trying to remember. As said before, if you're a kind person, your stories may need to be more violent in nature in order for you to remember them because a violent story would bring up new emotions and would fall outside your comfort zone. This inherently makes it not mundane, which leads to the quick recall of the information. If the stories above didn't connect with you, then it just means that you and I are made from different stock. That is completely fine. No two people are exactly alike, so it's impossible for one story to impact everyone in exactly the same way. In the end though, the method has been proven to work; you just need to figure out what kind of story works best for you.

Let's move on to the next five items in our Number-Rhyme Peg List.

| NUMBER | RHYME | REMEMBER THIS LIST |
|--------|-------|--------------------|
| 6 | Sticks | Clifford the Big Red Dog |
| 7 | Heaven | An Eel playing a Kazoo |
| 8 | Gate | Corn on the Cob |
| 9 | Wine | Garfield the Cat on the John |
| 10 | Hen | Gordon Ramsay with a Microphone |

Your Number-Rhyme peg for the number six is sticks, and the thing you're trying to remember is Clifford the Big Red Dog. We must now create an association between Clifford the Big Red Dog from the children's book/cartoons and some sticks. Once again, the simple association that will

37

*not* trigger any memory is to simply have Clifford fetch some sticks. It's understandable that would be the first thing to jump into your mind. So let's use it, but expand it so it becomes really interesting.

Imagine that you're walking through the park one afternoon and you hear a loud chainsaw grinding through trees up ahead. You jog to an area where there's a crowd of people standing and cheering. As you push your way to the front of the crowd, you see an amazing act taking place. There's a man high up in a tree with a chainsaw and he's cutting large branches off of the tree trunk. As the giant branches fall toward the ground, Clifford the Big Red Dog is leaping twenty feet into the air and biting them in his mouth before landing back on the ground.

Once he has a large branch in his jaws, he bites down hard, snapping it into smaller pieces. As the smaller pieces of the branches become sticks, he hits them with his paws and his tail, and the sticks fly toward a pile in the center of the crowd. The sticks that Clifford keeps chomping and hitting don't just land in a simple pile though. Clifford the Big Red Dog is an incredible artist and sculptor. The sticks fly in formation and land perfectly to form an odd house with four windows and a front and back door. The children run around laughing and are eager to play in the new stick house.

The chainsaw continues, the branches keep falling, and Clifford keeps swatting the sticks over to finish making the odd house. Finally, the chainsaw stops, the man climbs down, and he gets onto Clifford's back. They walk over to the stick house that Clifford constructed and they welcome all the children to play inside. As the kids run around, you look to your left and see Clifford rolling around in another pile of sticks. He's crushing them with his body, biting the sticks with his teeth, and shaping them into another structure.

When Clifford steps away from his work, you see that he's turned all of the sticks into an amazing jungle-gym with a climbing wall, a rope swing, monkey-bars, and an odd shaped slide. Clifford barks and everyone looks over to his new stick playground. All the kids rush from the house to the jungle-gym and start climbing, swinging, sliding, and playing around. You smile as the man and Clifford the Big Red Dog walk off down the road.

Now when you think of the number six, you should think of your Number-Rhyme peg of sticks and then quickly connect that to Clifford the Big Red Dog who's turning the sticks into an odd wooden house and a jungle-gym.

Your Number-Rhyme peg for the number seven is heaven, and the thing you're trying to remember is an eel playing a kazoo. We must now create an association between the image of heaven and an eel with a kazoo in his mouth.

38

Let's imagine that your time has come and you've passed on from this material world. It's sad, but you're at peace. You have no regrets. You've said goodbye to all your loved ones and you're now eagerly awaiting an eternity of bliss in heaven. You find yourself walking through the clouds toward the pearly gates. Everything is bright white and as peaceful as you imagined heaven would be.

As you walk closer to the gates of heaven, you see Saint Peter standing and talking with people in line in front of you. Sometimes you hear a pleasant ding of a chime and sometimes you hear a shocking sound and a harsh buzz. As you get closer to the front of the line, you see what's happening. After a brief conversation with the person, Saint Peter either rings the chime and the person enters heaven or a massive electric eel sends out a lightning bolt at the person, buzzes his large tin kazoo, and the person falls from heaven straight into hell.

The eel is a complete villain. He's laughing and enjoying zapping people and buzzing his kazoo before sending the person to hell. The peaceful feeling you had just before has vanished as you get closer to the front of the line. You think back to all the bad things you've ever done in your life and wonder if you'll be judged favorably or if you'll spend an eternity in hell. The woman two persons ahead of you approaches Saint Peter, and after only a few seconds, the giant electric eel raises up, zaps her with a lightning bolt, blows his kazoo, and she falls from heaven. The man in front of you steps forward and you can almost hear the words being spoken. You wait for the pleasant chime, but it doesn't come. Again, the eel slithers around, jumps up, extends his tail, shoots lightning at the man, and blows into his kazoo. You hear the buzzing of the kazoo and its vibrations shake you at your core. The man disappears as he falls below.

You take a deep breath and step forward. You're so nervous and continue to pray that you'll be one of the lucky ones to spend an eternity in heaven. The eel is slithering around at your feet with the kazoo in his mouth, drooling at the chance to send another human to hell. Saint Peter looks at his scroll and asks you, "Do you believe you have earned the right to enter heaven?" You close your eyes and say, "Yes, I do." Then there's silence. You're waiting for the chime. You fear the harsh buzz of the kazoo. You feel the eel slither through your legs one last time, and as you open your eyes to learn your fate, you see Saint Peter ring the chime and welcome you into heaven. You exhale all your fear and walk past the gates and into heaven. As the gates close behind you, you hear the eel buzz his kazoo once again and are grateful for your good fortune.

Now when you think of the number seven, you'll see your Number-Rhyme peg heaven, and then as you tell yourself the story above, you'll easily recall the eel playing a kazoo.

39

Your Number-Rhyme peg for the number eight is a gate, and the thing you're trying to remember is corn on the cob. We must now create an association between a gate and some kind of corn on the cob. Let's make this story short and full of action. The more action there is, the more excitement there usually is too. Where there's excitement, there's interest and remember that interest is critical in the memorization process. Imagine you're in Nebraska at the county fair. It's evening and everyone is lining up for the fireworks show. The crowd all rushes over to the field and sits down on blankets and lawn chairs. In front of everyone is a long white picket fence with an intricately designed wrought iron gate. The gate has metal cobs of corn twisting along its perimeter as well as through the middle. The fireworks show in Nebraska is unique because they use dried corn on the cob as the rockets that shoot up into the sky.

In order to trigger the launching mechanism to shoot the corn on the cob into the air, the fireworks specialist opens and then slams the wrought iron gate shut with a massive push that causes sparks to shoot off the gate's handle and ignite the corn. There are at least one thousand stalks of corn on the cob leaning against the gate and you know it's going to be an exciting show. The corn cobs are stacked neatly and separated by colors. The blue and yellow cobs are leaning on the right side of the gate, while the red and green cobs are leaning on the left side of the gate.

The show begins. The gate is opened, several corn on the cobs are placed against the lock, and the gate is slammed shut. You see the spark, hear the sizzle of the wick, and watch in amazement as the corn on the cob that was leaning on the gate shoots into the night sky and explodes into brilliant colors. Again and again, the cobs shoot from the gate into the sky and explode. The best part about the corn-on-the-cob fireworks is that everyone has a pillowcase with them to catch all of the popcorn as it floats down from the sky. A million pieces of blue, red, green, and yellow popped corn fall gently back to earth. You open your pillowcase and your mouth to catch as much of the popped corn as possible.

So when you think of your Number-Rhyme peg for the number eight, you'll think of the corn on the cob leaning against the gate.

Your Number-Rhyme peg for the number nine is wine, and the thing you're trying to remember is Garfield the Cat on the john. We must now create an association between a bottle of wine and Garfield the Cat sitting on a toilet. This one should be fun to create. Imagine you come home after a long day. You flop down on the couch to relax for a few minutes before grabbing something to eat. As you relax with your eyes closed, you hear a loud crash coming from the bathroom. You jump up from the couch and sprint to the bathroom door. Inside you hear scratching, gulping, burping, and something that sounds like a groaning meow. You place your hand on the doorknob and slowly turn it to the right. You gently push the door open and peek your head inside, expecting to find a burglar smashing your medicine cabinet.

As the door opens, you're shocked to find Garfield the Cat sitting on the toilet with his legs spread open, scratching his belly, and chugging a bottle of red wine. He raises the bottle to his mouth, takes a massive gulp, wipes the Merlot dripping from his lips, belches, and scratches his belly again. You don't know what to do. It's the most insane thing you've ever seen. You shake your head to try to wake yourself because you think you must be dreaming, but it's real. Garfield the Cat is sitting on your john getting drunk on red wine!

Garfield swigs the last bit of wine and hurls the bottle at the wall. It falls to the floor in a thousand shards of tinted glass. Garfield reaches under the toilet and pulls out another bottle of red wine. He uses his claw as a corkscrew and pops the cork out of the bottle. He flicks the cork from his paw, raises the bottle to his mouth, tilts his neck back, and chugs the entire bottle. He finishes the wine in a few seconds, throws the bottle against the wall again, belches, scratches his belly, and then reaches behind himself to flush the toilet. He looks at you and says, "Hey, get me more Merlot, would you?" You close the door, shake your head, and walk back to the couch. You lie down, close your eyes, and pray it's all just a dream.

What a funny story that links the Number-Rhyme peg for nine, wine, to Garfield the Cat on the john. Of course this would never happen, but that's the point. Our mind remembers things that are out of the ordinary and seeing Garfield the Cat chugging wine on the toilet is anything but ordinary.

Your Number-Rhyme peg for the number ten is hen, and the thing you're trying to remember is Gordon Ramsay with a microphone. We must now create an association between a hen and Gordon Ramsay holding a microphone. The logical thing would be to picture Gordon Ramsay holding a microphone and talking into it as he prepares a hen for dinner. Since this is actually something very plausible for Gordon Ramsay to do, there's nothing unique or interesting about it. We've seen the same thing from him on television many times. In order to make the link memorable, Gordon Ramsay needs to be doing something unheard of with the microphone and the hen. Can you picture Gordon Ramsay in the hen house trying to capture a hen to prepare for dinner? Let's build on that.

Imagine that Gordon enters the henhouse looking for the perfect hen to prepare for dinner. He reaches down to grab a plump hen, but it runs to the other side of the building. He tries to grab another hen, but that one also escapes. He tries a third time, but still cannot grab a hen with his hands. He appears to be wearing a gun holster, but instead of a gun on his hip, there's a silver microphone with a long cord. He takes the microphone out of the holster and swings it around and around from the cord. The

41

length of the cord grows and the microphone at the end picks up speed. He aims carefully and with one strong rotation, he whacks one of the hens right in the gut. The hen flies across the henhouse and smashes into the opposite wall. The hen is stunned, but still alive. The hen stumbles around, shakes his head, looks up at Gordon and says, "What did you do that for, you big bully?"

Gordon replies, "I need a volunteer to be dinner tonight and you look yummy." With that, the hen leaps into the air and flies right at Gordon's face. He raises the microphone, swings it around and around again, but instead of the microphone hitting the hen, the cord wraps around his torso and his legs. He falls to the ground completely tied up by the microphone cord. All of the hens slowly approach Gordon and begin pecking at him. He shakes, screams, and flails around on the ground until he wriggles himself out of the microphone cord. He runs out of the henhouse and slams the door shut behind him. The hen peeks its head out of the window and says, "Never come back again."

Now when you think of the hen, which is the Number-Rhyme peg for the number ten, you'll think of Gordon Ramsay with a microphone. I know that some of these stories were violent. I'm certainly not supporting animal cruelty in any way. My personality is actually quite passive. I shy away from violence in my life, so when I create violent stories for my associations, they stand out to me and are memorable because they contain action, uncomfortable emotions, and things that are opposite of the way I behave in my life. These all add up to a story that is interesting, which compels me to remember it easier. As mentioned before, if the stories presented here don't interest you, then you must create your own stories that work for the way you think.

It's time for another break before we see how much information you've retained. Please close the book. Do something completely unrelated to memory training and try not to think about all of the silly stories from this section. Let yourself relax. When you come back, you'll run through the stories to see how much information you remember. Go on and close the book now.

●●●●●●●●

Welcome back from your break. The more breaks you take, the more starts and stops you create, and by the natural way your brain works, you'll retain more information.

It's time now to see how well you've applied the Number-Rhyme Peg List technique. Take a few minutes to tell yourself the stories that link the Number-Rhyme image presented below to the thing you're trying to remember. Either fill in the spaces below or just recall them all in your head. It may help to retell yourself the story out loud. The more you make the stories your own, the faster you'll master the technique and the quicker you'll remember the information. Make sure not to turn the pages backward or forward. If you cheat by sneaking a look at the filled-in list on the other pages, you won't be melting that ball of wax on top of your head. You'll just be short-changing yourself and slowing down your progress.

| NUMBER | RHYME | REMEMBER THIS LIST |
|:---:|:---:|:---:|
| 1 | Sun | |
| 2 | Shoe | |
| 3 | Tree | |
| 4 | Door | |
| 5 | Hive | |
| 6 | Sticks | |
| 7 | Heaven | |
| 8 | Gate | |
| 9 | Wine | |
| 10 | Hen | |

●●●●●●●●

How did you do? Here is the complete list you were asked to memorize.

| NUMBER | RHYME | REMEMBER THIS LIST |
|---|---|---|
| 1 | Sun | Hairy Clergyman |
| 2 | Shoe | Crawfish Shells |
| 3 | Tree | Straws made from Leaves |
| 4 | Door | Steel Adding Machine |
| 5 | Hive | Sand in my Eyes |
| 6 | Sticks | Clifford the Big Red Dog |
| 7 | Heaven | An Eel playing a Kazoo |
| 8 | Gate | Corn on the Cob |
| 9 | Wine | Garfield the Cat on the John |
| 10 | Hen | Gordon Ramsay with a Microphone |

Did you get all ten? If you really retold yourself the stories and vividly pictured them in your mind's eye, I'm sure you easily named all ten. Turn the page again and be sure not to look forward or backward. Really challenge yourself to work through the exercise honestly.

Let's have fun with this list to show how you can recall this information inside and out, forward and backward, and in a random order. Again, make sure not to look at the list as you go through this exercise.

- What number and rhyme image do you think of when you read *corn on the cob*?
- What do you remember when you read the Number-Rhyme *sun*?
- What do you remember when you read the Number-Rhyme *sticks*?
- What number and rhyme image do you think of when you read *an eel playing a kazoo?*
- What number and rhyme image do you think of when you read *steel adding machine*?
- What do you remember when you read the Number-Rhyme *hive*?
- What number and rhyme image do you think of when you read *Gordon Ramsay with a microphone*?
- What number and rhyme image do you think of when you read *Straws made from leaves*?
- What do you remember when you read the Number-Rhyme *shoe*?
- What do you remember when you read the Number-Rhyme *wine*?

Did you get them all? Isn't it amazing that you now have a number-rhyme peg list of ten images that you can peg any new information to and can recall in any order instantly? This is a powerful tool that you'll use to help memorize your lines.

Why were you asked to recall these ten crazy images? What does the silly list have to do with acting? Well, without you knowing it, you've just remembered the names of ten of the founding members of The Group Theatre that was formed in the early 1930s. By changing the actor's name into an image, I pegged the image to the Number-Rhyme peg, and by getting back to the image that was associated to the Number-Rhyme peg, I can recall the names of the founders.

| NUMBER | RHYME | IMAGES TO REMEMBER | FOUNDING MEMBERS OF THE GROUP THEATRE |
|--------|-------|--------------------|----------------------------------------|
| 1 | Sun | Hairy Clergyman | Harold Clurman |
| 2 | Shoe | Crawfish Shells | Cheryl Crawford |
| 3 | Tree | Straws made from Leaves | Lee Strasberg |
| 4 | Door | Steel Adding Machine | Stella Adler |
| 5 | Hive | Sand in my Eyes | Sandy Meisner |
| 6 | Sticks | Clifford the Big Red Dog | Clifford Odets |
| 7 | Heaven | An Eel playing a Kazoo | Elia Kazan |
| 8 | Gate | Corn on the Cob | Lee J. Cobb |
| 9 | Wine | Garfield the Cat on the John | John Garfield |
| 10 | Hen | Gordon Ramsay with a Microphone | Michael Gordon |

I took the name Harold Clurman and turned that into a hairy clergyman. Can you see how I got from Harold Clurman to hairy clergyman? When I retell myself the story of the sun igniting the hairy clergyman, I can easily get back to Harold Clurman. The same holds true for how I turned Cheryl Crawford into Crawfish Shells. Once I remember the crawfish shells in my shoes, I'll remember Cheryl Crawford.

Lee Strasberg was turned into straws made from leaves. Leaves equals Lee and straws equals Strasberg. The steel adding machine is my image for Stella Adler. The image of sand in my eyes is my image for Sandy Meisner.

Clifford Odets was changed into Clifford the Big Red Dog making the odd shaped house. The image in heaven of the eel playing the kazoo reminds me of Elia Kazan. The eel is for Elia and the kazoo is for Kazan. The corn on the cob leaning against the gate takes me back to Lee J. Cobb.

Garfield on the toilet, which I'm calling the john in this example, makes me remember John Garfield and the microphone in Gordon Ramsay's hand as he attacks the poor hens makes me remember Michael Gordon.

By turning the person's name into an image and then associating it to the Number-Rhyme peg list, you can easily remember the founding members of one of the most important theatre groups to ever be created in the world. These founding members took what they learned from Constantin Stanislavski and developed amazing acting techniques that every actor should explore. Regardless of whether you're in the Meisner camp, the Strasberg camp, the Adler camp, or any other camp, knowing the history of acting and how the techniques were developed will add to your acting knowledge base.

The bonus here is that in addition to learning techniques for remembering your lines, you've just learned the method for remembering people's names, which is something many people struggle with. As shown above, you must turn the names into an image in order to remember it. As discussed before, our mind thinks in pictures not in words, so if you simply try to remember a name, you're trying to remember a word and you'll likely fail. There are other elements to remembering people's names that fall outside the purpose of this book, but for completeness, here are the basic steps:

- **Step 1:** Listen to their name when the other person introduces themselves. All too often, we don't even give the other person the courtesy of listening when they say their name.
- **Step 2:** Use your imagination to turn their name into an image. Creating standards will help speed this process up. Examples are all men named Chris will be turned into the image of a cross. All men named Michael will be turned into a microphone. All men named Mark will be turned into a magic marker. All women named Carol will be turned into coral. All women named Beth will be turned into a bathtub. All women named Debbie will be turned into a bee. These are just examples of images, but as mentioned before, you should create your own to speed up the process.
- **Step 3:** Find a unique facial feature on the person's face that will never go away. It's important that you don't pick something like their glasses because they may be wearing contact lenses the next time you see them. Pick their nose, a mole, their dimples, a lazy eye, a scar, their bald head, their bright blue eyes, their eyebrows, etc.
- **Step 4:** Peg the image of their name to the facial feature in some crazy way. So if you meet a man named Michael who has a big nose, you'd listen to his name, turn Michael into a microphone, and then imagine jamming a microphone into his nose so hard that it gets completely stuck inside his nose.

The wackier you make the story, the easier it will be to remember their name. Remember, never tell the other person *how* you remember their

47

name. It's none of their business that you've just smashed a microphone into their nose in your mind. All they need to know is that you cared enough about them to remember their name.

Okay, it's time for another break. Close the book and come back when you're rested.

●●●●●●●●

# THE NUMBER-ASSOCIATION PEG LIST
# THE NUMBER-SHAPE PEG LIST

At this point, I'm sure you're eager to learn how to apply the techniques to remembering monologues and dialogues. We're almost there—there are just a few more layers that need to be added onto the technique. In the previous section, you learned about the Number-Rhyme Peg List. Obviously, this list is based on your peg images rhyming with their corresponding number. The peg image of the sun rhymes with the number one, the peg image of a door rhymes with the number four. And so on.

There are two other number peg lists that you can use. The first is the Number-Association Peg List and the second is the Number-Shape Peg List. Later in the book when we get to the section on remembering dialogues, we'll use the Number-Association Peg List. To help accelerate the memorization process later, it's highly recommended that you use these two peg lists right now to practice the "pegging" of crazy stories on your own. By doing the next two sections on your own, you'll help yourself advance to a more competent level.

If you're concerned that you're not "doing it right" or if you get stuck and need some guidance, I am just an email away. I would be glad to review your stories and help you make them even more memorable. To contact me, please either visit my website, www.jaredkelner.com and go to the "Submit Your Peg List" section or simply email me at jared@jaredkelner.com. Be sure to tell me which peg list you're using, what you're trying to remember, and what your crazy story is. I'll review it and reply back with suggestions as soon as possible.

Below are the three number peg lists. The rhyme column is the one we've already covered. The association and the shape columns are the sections we'll explore now.

| NUMBER | RHYME | ASSOCIATION | SHAPE |
|--------|-------|-------------|-------|
| 1 | Sun (Bun, Gun) | Unicycle | Candle |
| 2 | Shoe (Glue, Zoo) | Bicycle | Swan |
| 3 | Tree (Bee, Tea) | Tricycle | Heart |
| 4 | Door (Boar, Shore) | Car | Sail |
| 5 | Hive (Dive, Drive) | Glove | Fish Hook |
| 6 | Sticks (Bricks, Tricks) | Six-pack of Soda | Elephant's Trunk |
| 7 | Heaven | Pair of Dice | Boomerang |
| 8 | Gate (Bait, Crate) | Roller Skates | Snowman |
| 9 | Wine (Sign, Vine) | Cat | Balloon on a String |
| 10 | Hen (Men, Pen) | Bowling | Bat and Ball |

In the grid below are images that have an association to their number. In other words, the peg has some specific attribute that makes you think of the number it's linked to.

| NUMBER | ASSOCIATION | REMEMBER THIS LIST |
|:------:|:-----------:|:------------------:|
| 1 | Unicycle | |
| 2 | Bicycle | |
| 3 | Tricycle | |
| 4 | Car | |
| 5 | Glove | |
| 6 | Six-pack of Soda | |
| 7 | Pair of Dice | |
| 8 | Roller Skates | |
| 9 | Cat | |
| 10 | Bowling | |

For the number one, the unicycle is the association image because it only has one wheel. For example, if you needed to remember bananas as your first item, you would create some crazy story with a banana interacting with a unicycle. Remember, it's not just a banana riding a unicycle, but rather something crazy, like a unicycle made out of banana peels that causes the rider to slip and fall and land in a pile of banana pudding.

For the number two, a bicycle is the association image because it has two wheels. If you needed to remember light bulbs, you could create a story about riding your bicycle so fast that the electrical wires connected to your chain help generate the power needed to light up the light bulbs in your house. But perhaps you pedal too fast and the light bulbs burst.

Your association image for the number three is a tricycle because a tricycle has three wheels. Your association image for the number four is a car because a car has four wheels. Your association image for the number five is a glove because a glove has five fingers. Your association image for the number six is a six-pack of soda because a six-pack of soda has six cans. Your association image for the number seven is a pair of dice because a pair of dice is used in the game craps and you try to roll lucky number seven. Your association image for the number eight is roller skates because roller skates have eight wheels. Your association image for the number nine is a cat because a cat has nine lives. Finally, your association image for the number ten is bowling because bowling has ten frames, ten pins, and a strike has a value of ten.

Why don't you take some time to write down a list of ten things you wish to remember and then peg them to your Number-Association Peg List?

| NUMBER | ASSOCIATION | REMEMBER THIS LIST |
|:------:|:-----------:|:------------------:|
| 1 | Unicycle | |
| 2 | Bicycle | |
| 3 | Tricycle | |
| 4 | Car | |
| 5 | Glove | |
| 6 | Six-pack of Soda | |
| 7 | Pair of Dice | |
| 8 | Roller Skates | |
| 9 | Cat | |
| 10 | Bowling | |

In the grid below are images whose shapes closely resemble the number itself when it is written. In other words, the peg physically looks like the number that it's linked to.

| NUMBER | SHAPE | REMEMBER THIS LIST |
|:------:|:-----:|:------------------:|
| 1 | Candle | |
| 2 | Swan | |
| 3 | Heart | |
| 4 | Sail | |
| 5 | Fish Hook | |
| 6 | Elephant's Trunk | |
| 7 | Boomerang | |
| 8 | Snowman | |
| 9 | Balloon on a String | |
| 10 | Bat and Ball | |

For the number one, the candle is the shape image because a candle is a straight object that stands tall just like the number one. If you needed to remember to fill your car with gasoline, then you might create a story of you pouring gasoline onto a giant candle and watching as the flame grows

51

high and the wax from the candle melts so much that you get swept away in a river of melted wax.

For the number two, a swan is the shape image because a swan swimming on a lake with its neck curved looks just like the number two. If you needed to remember to buy eggs, maybe you could create a story about a swan swimming like a maniac on a lake and shooting eggs out at all the people trying to row their boats. Remember to have fun with the stories and make them interesting to you.

Your shape image for the number three is a heart because the top of the heart has two bumps just like the number three. Your shape image for the number four is a sail on a boat. A sail unfurled on a mast and blowing in the wind looks like the number four. Your shape image for the number five is a fish hook because a fish hook has the same curved lines as the number five. Your shape image for the number six is an elephant's trunk because an elephant's trunk looks just like the number six. Your shape image for the number seven is a boomerang. Some people like to use the image of a cliff for the number seven, but I prefer the boomerang because your stories with a boomerang are typically filled with more action than stories about a cliff. If you can make your stories about a cliff exciting to you, try using a cliff instead of a boomerang. In either case, both the boomerang and a cliff look like the number seven.

Your shape image for the number eight is a snowman. You could also use the image of a sand-filled hour glass. Both images look like the number eight and both will work well. Your shape image for the number nine is a balloon on a string. Finally, your shape image for the number ten is a bat and ball. The bat would be the number one and the ball would be the zero. Stand the bat up next to the ball and you have what looks like the number ten. Other shape options for the number ten are the comedy duos of Laurel and Hardy or Abbott and Costello.

If you didn't try using the Number-Association Peg List to make up your own stories for a list of ten things you've come up with, you should try using this Number-Shape Peg List. Even better would be to try both and make up twenty stories about twenty new things you wish to recall. Remember that if you'd like me to provide some feedback or guidance on your attempts to apply the techniques, please contact me through my website, www.jaredkelner.com and go to the "Submit Your Peg List" section or simply email me at jared@jaredkelner.com. Be sure to tell me which peg list you're using, what you're trying to remember, and what your crazy story is. I'll review it and reply with suggestions as soon as possible.

Often, people ask if the peg lists can be reused and if yes, how you prevent one list from overlapping into another list. The answer is yes, you certainly can have multiple lists of information pegged to the same peg list.

You'll have to try it to experience it for yourself. Your brain will remember what items belong to which list, but to help you be certain, when you're first starting out, the second time you use the same peg list to associate new information, consider adding an attribute to every story.

For example, in your second list, everything would be the same color, or everything would be frozen in ice, or everything would be covered in feathers, or everything would be exploding, and so on. By putting a common attribute on the second set of things you're pegging to the same list, you help your mind segment them, which will make the information easier to recall. Over time, though, you'll discover that you don't need to apply the common attribute to your new list and you'll still remember the new information without mixing it up with previous lists.

Before we take a break, let's see if you can shift from the Number Peg Lists back to the Link/Chain Method. Tell yourself the story from the earlier section and then fill in the names of Shakespeare's plays below. Don't cheat by looking ahead.

## Shakespeare's Comedies

- _____
- _____
- _____
- _____
- _____
- _____
- _____
- _____
- _____
- _____
- _____
- _____
- _____
- _____

How did you do? Is it getting easier? Here is the list again so you can see how well you did. Again, if you missed anything, it's because you probably rushed past the details of the story to try to get to the answer or because the story itself didn't truly interest you. If either was the case, take your time to expand on the story so that it's meaningful to you. When you retell it to yourself, take time to relive every detail to activate your senses as much as possible.

## <u>Shakespeare's Comedies</u>

- All's Well That Ends Well
- As You Like It
- The Comedy of Errors
- Love's Labour's Lost
- Measure for Measure
- The Merchant of Venice
- The Merry Wives of Windsor
- A Midsummer Night's Dream
- Much Ado About Nothing
- The Taming of the Shrew
- The Tempest
- Twelfth Night
- Two Gentlemen of Verona
- The Winter's Tale

Okay, it's time again to take a break. Make sure it's a longer break this time because when you come back you need to be fresh and ready to learn. In the next section, we'll apply these techniques to remembering a monologue. Take your break now.

●●●●●●●●

# SECTION 3: MEMORIZING MONOLOGUES

## THE ROOM PEG LIST

You've learned a tremendous amount so far and all of your hard work is about to pay off. Picture yourself at the top of a giant roller coaster. You climbed and climbed and now you're at the apex about to enjoy the exhilarating ride down.

All of the time that you spent learning how to peg images and how to make your stories memorable need to be leveraged and expanded upon in the coming sections. Although new techniques will be presented, the foundation principles you've learned still apply. The first of three methods for memorizing a monologue will be taught through the Room Peg List. We'll then move onto the Journey Method and after that the Body Peg List. Just like we used images that rhymed with numbers, images that had an association to the number, and images that had the same physical shape as the number it represented, we can essentially turn anything into a peg list. The more peg lists you create, the more options you have available for remembering new information. To explore our first monologue, we're going to use The Room Peg List.

To create a Room Peg List, you must mentally put yourself in the middle of a room at your house or in a room someplace that you're very familiar with. This room should have four walls and four corners, and should contain furniture and items around the perimeter of the room. If there's a bare wall or a corner with nothing in it, you'll learn how to use that too, but the more objects there are in the room, the better your Room Peg List will be.

To start, you must designate ten locations in your room that will become your pegs. The ten room pegs will be situated in a circle around the room. Remember to stand in the middle of the room facing whichever direction feels the most forward-facing to you. On the next page you'll find the ten locations:

## The Room Peg List Locations

1. The back corner over your left shoulder
2. The side wall as you look left
3. The far left corner in front of you
4. The wall straight in front of you
5. The far right corner in front of you
6. The side wall as you look right
7. The back corner over your right shoulder
8. The back wall behind you
9. The floor in the middle of the room
10. The ceiling

Now that you have the ten locations designated, look at what objects or furniture are in each location. For the purposes of this exercise, I'm going to create an imaginary room filled with objects, but once you're done with this section, it will be very important for you to create your own Room Peg List with a room and objects in that room that you're very familiar with. Also note that the more rooms you use, the more peg lists you'll have, so once you create, use, and master one Room Peg List, you should consider making every room in your house into a Room Peg List.

To help with memorizing the monologue that will be presented shortly, let's imagine that the items in **(BOLD)** that are written next to the ten locations are the objects in this imaginary room that we'll use as our pegs.

1. The back corner over your left shoulder **(UPRIGHT PIANO)**
2. The side wall as you look left **(OVERSTUFFED COUCH)**
3. The far left corner in front of you **(WOODEN BOOKCASE)**
4. The wall straight in front of you **(FLAT SCREEN TELEVISION)**
5. The far right corner in front of you **(WURLITZER JUKEBOX)**
6. The side wall as you look right **(LARGE WINDOW)**
7. The back corner over your right shoulder **(WOODEN COMPUTER HUTCH)**
8. The back wall behind you **(LIGHT PANEL WITH FOUR SWITCHES)**
9. The floor in the middle of the room **(GLASS COFFEE TABLE)**
10. The ceiling **(FOUR BLADE CEILING FAN)**

Let's try something different here. Take out a piece of paper and draw a large square on the paper. If possible, use colored pencils or markers for this exercise. Then, as best you can, draw a picture of each of the ten objects above in **(BOLD)**. The artwork doesn't need to be good. It just needs to be good enough for you to know what it is. Don't just write the words down in their locations. The act of drawing helps to spark the creative process and that will help manufacture interest because it will be something you've created.

Take a few minutes to draw the piano, couch, bookcase, television, jukebox, window, computer hutch, light panel, coffee table, and ceiling fan around your room.

Did you use colored pencils or markers? Remember that our mind thinks in pictures and we don't think in black and white. The more colorful your pictures are, the more active they become, which will make your peg list more interesting. Have fun with this. When else in your life are you asked to draw ten silly pictures?

Now that you have your Room Peg List colored to the best of your ability, set the paper down. Below is the simple monologue you'll be asked to memorize. We'll walk through the process every step of the way. As you read on and work through the exercise, make sure to take your time and let your imagination run wild. Remember that as an actor, your creative mind is one of your most important assets. Leverage it as much as possible. Here is the first of your three monologues:

The moon was full and the rain poured down like cats and dogs.
I stood alone on the beach and watched the waves crash in the distance.
Lightning danced across the night sky and I thought I could see heaven.
Max barked and dropped a wet tennis ball at my feet.
I sipped my coffee and dreamed of flying away.

It's a very short and simple piece, but perfect for our exercise. There are two approaches to this process. The first is to simply memorize the lines without any consideration to what emotions, actions, obstacles, and objectives will be used when performing the piece. The second is to integrate the memory technique as you're developing the piece from a performance perspective. Both approaches work very well. It's simply a matter of personal preference.

To demonstrate the power of integrating the memorization process with the acting technique of emotionally breaking down the script, I'll demonstrate how to do both at the same time in this exercise.

Let's develop this from an acting technique perspective. We have nothing more than the monologue itself to go on, so we know nothing about the character or what's happening, which means we must create our own back story. Regardless of which acting school or technique you're coming from, what I'll present here is universal to the acting process. Let's create the back story to determine what just happened and where you just came from.

Here is the monologue again.

The moon was full and the rain poured down like cats and dogs.
I stood alone on the beach and watched the waves crash in the distance.
Lightning danced across the night sky and I thought I could see heaven.
Max barked and dropped a wet tennis ball at my feet.
I sipped my coffee and dreamed of flying away.

Imagine that your ten-year relationship with the love of your life just ended. Your loved one passed away after a nine-month battle with cancer. You stood by her side and helped the nurse care for her every day. Bathing and dressing her. Feeding and administering medication to her. You were there when they hung the morphine bag to help your loved one slip into a coma and finally pass on. Tomorrow morning is the funeral, but tonight you've come to the beach where you first met ten years ago.

On the sand, you've laid out the old blanket that kept your loved one warm for the past nine months. You brought along a thermos full of the hazelnut coffee you shared every morning. Your beloved golden retriever, Max, is running around the beach with his favorite tennis ball in his mouth, unaware that life will never be the same. The skies open up, and as the rain pours down on you, you stand alone and pray that the ocean will carry your pain out to sea.

Above is a touching back story to help define who you are, what just happened, where you are, where you're going, what you want, what's in your way, and how you feel. As an actor, you now need to explore choices of how you want to approach this from an emotional preparation perspective. Will you prepare for sadness or rage or some other emotion? That part is up to you. My suggestion is to try a variety of approaches during the rehearsal process and to determine which one you connect most closely to. For the purposes of this exercise, let's use sadness instead of rage. This emotional choice will help color and shape the stories we create when we apply the Room Peg List to the monologue.

Before we begin, it's critically important to discuss what typically happens when actors forget their lines. From personal experience as an actor and an acting teacher and confirmed by research, I've learned that when an actor forgets his lines, it's usually not because he can't remember the specific words that come next. Rather, he can't recall the next thought or topic in the script. Once he hears the first few words of the line or is given a clue as to the general topic of the next section of the script, the light bulb turns on and the words come flowing back.

The issue is that the actor is struggling to connect to the next thought, the next topic, and the next image, not that he can't remember the actual words on the page. So once he connects with the image that represents the next thought in the script, he will remember the words. This is demonstrated when an actor forgets what words come next and calls, "Line?" Moments after he hears the first few words of his next line read by someone offstage, he says, "I remember now," motions to the person reading from the script to stop talking and continues saying his monologue or dialogue. The actor simply needed to hear a few words to trigger the image of the next thought in his monologue and once he locked onto that next thought, he was able to complete his line.

The next step in the process is to break down the script into images. Remember that we don't think in words, we think in pictures. To memorize the monologue, we must identify the key thoughts throughout the piece and turn them into images. Once we have an image, we can peg it to our Room Peg List object. Keep the paper that you drew of your Room Peg List handy to help you visualize this imaginary room. Let's break the monologue down into images or thoughts now. Below, I've underlined and made bold the words in the monologue that create images.

The **moon was full** and the **rain poured down like cats and dogs**.
I **stood alone on the beach** and watched the **waves crash** in the distance.
**Lightning danced** across the night sky and I thought I could see **heaven**.
**Max barked** and **dropped a wet tennis ball** at my feet.
I **sipped my coffee** and **dreamed of flying away**.

The next step is to turn the words or thoughts from the monologue into strong images that you then peg or associate in some memorable way to the objects or locations in your Room Peg List. Just as we pegged the hairy clergyman to the Number-Rhyme peg of the sun to eventually help us remember Harold Clurman, here too, you'll peg the images pulled from the monologue to the objects around your room. Once the stories are created, as you go around the room in your mind's eye, you'll see the object you've designated as your peg, then you'll see the interaction of the monologue's image with your room peg, and that will help get you back to the line you're trying to remember. Since we're going to integrate the emotional preparation of sadness into our stories, as you read on, pay attention to how the association stories we create will help you when you perform the piece because they will connect you to the emotion you're preparing for.

A side note: Some actors will prepare for emotions using actual experiences from their lives that evoked a similar emotional response as what is needed for the scene. Other actors believe that using your personal experiences is limiting and instead throw themselves into the imaginary world created by the playwright and use their imagination to believe the given circumstances in order to bring themselves to a heightened emotional state. The memory technique will work equally well regardless of your acting method or approach. In the end, your job as an actor is to bring the character to life and to deliver a believable and meaningful performance. How you get there and what acting technique you use is irrelevant, and nobody's business anyway. That same principle applies to memory techniques. What goes on in your head to help you remember your lines is nobody's business and should not be shared. The more you make things personal, the stronger your connection to the thing you're trying to recall will be and the results will speak for themselves.

Before we create the stories, let's remind ourselves what we'll be pegging.

1. The back corner over your left shoulder **(UPRIGHT PIANO)**
   - *We will peg an image of the full moon to the upright piano*
2. The side wall as you look left **(OVERSTUFFED COUCH)**
   - *We will peg an image of the rain pouring down like cats and dogs to the overstuffed couch*
3. The far left corner in front of you **(WOODEN BOOKCASE)**
   - *We will peg an image of you standing alone on the beach to the wooden bookcase*
4. The wall straight in front of you **(FLAT SCREEN TELEVISION)**
   - *We will peg an image of the waves crashing in the distance to the flat screen television*
5. The far right corner in front of you **(WURLITZER JUKEBOX)**
   - *We will peg an image of lightning dancing across the night sky to the Wurlitzer jukebox*
6. The side wall as you look right **(LARGE WINDOW)**
   - *We will peg an image of heaven to the large window*
7. The back corner over your right shoulder **(WOODEN COMPUTER HUTCH)**
   - *We will peg an image of Max the dog barking to the wooden computer hutch*
8. The back wall behind you **(LIGHT PANEL WITH FOUR SWITCHES)**
   - *We will peg an image of the wet tennis ball being dropped at your feet to the light panel with four switches*
9. The floor in the middle of the room **(GLASS COFFEE TABLE)**
   - *We will peg an image of you drinking your coffee to the glass coffee table*
10. The ceiling **(FOUR BLADE CEILING FAN)**
    - *We will peg an image of you flying away to the four blade ceiling fan*

Take a moment to reread the back story created to help with the memorization and acting process. Imagine that your ten-year relationship with the love of your life just ended. Your loved one passed away after a nine-month battle with cancer. You stood by her side and helped the nurse care for her every day. Bathing and dressing her. Feeding and administering medication to her. You were there when they hung the morphine bag to help your loved one slip into a coma and finally pass on. Tomorrow morning is the funeral, but tonight you've come to the beach where you first met ten years ago.

On the sand, you've laid out the old blanket that kept your loved one warm for the past nine months. You brought along a thermos full of the hazelnut coffee you shared every morning. Your beloved golden retriever, Max, is running around the beach with his favorite tennis ball in his mouth, unaware that life will never be the same. The skies open up, and as the rain pours down on you, you stand alone and pray that the ocean will carry your pain out to sea.

Let's begin. Imagine that you're standing in the middle of your room. You look over your left shoulder toward the upright piano and see a massive full moon playing the piano. The full moon is glowing a gentle shade of blue and sadly singing the song *Blue Moon* by the band The Marcels. The moon is wearing a black tuxedo and appears to be weeping as he's singing. You sing along with the full moon and a lump forms in your throat as you sing about standing alone without your love.

When you visualize the piano, the image of the sad full moon should quickly come to mind. The somber mood that the moon sets and the sad song he sings will help you connect to the emotion that you believe to be appropriate when delivering the line, "The moon was full."

You now look to the wall to your left and see the overstuffed couch. Let's imagine that pouring down from the sky are thousands of cats and dogs. There are two soaking wet cats clawing and biting each other as they flail around on the couch in a violent rage. There are sopping wet dogs huddled together on the couch trying to keep each other warm, but the rain is making them shiver. There are angry dogs chasing frightened cats around the couch and splashing through the puddles. There are shivering cats standing under protective dogs to shield themselves from the cold rain. The cats and dogs continue to pour down from the sky and have completely covered the overstuffed couch.

The different actions of the cats and dogs will help tie back to the multiple emotions you as an actor are portraying while delivering the line, "and the rain poured down like cats and dogs." Even though you're preparing for one emotion—sadness—to start the monologue, you must let your emotions go where they want to go. In this case, with the back story we've created, it makes perfect sense that there could be competing emotions of sadness, anger, fear, guilt, or shame when you perform the monologue.

Next, you should look ahead to the far left corner of your room where the wooden bookcase stands. Imagine the bookcase is fragile, old, rickety, dusty, tilted, and unstable. Picture the bookcase standing at an angle in sand at the beach. See yourself slowly and carefully climbing up the bookcase. As you step on each shelf, you feel the brittle wood bend beneath your feet. You pull yourself up to the top of the bookcase and, like a circus performer standing on a tightrope, you balance on top of the tilting, teetering structure. Once you gain your footing, you look down to see the ocean water rushing in and splashing the bottom of the bookcase. As the tide rushes out, sand is pulled away from the base of the bookcase and it begins to rock back and forth. You feel your body being pulled forward and backward and you try desperately to stand, but can't stop the bookcase from crashing down to the sand. You tumble through the air, but somehow land on your feet. You stand alone in the sand as the waves rush cold water around your legs.

The rocking and uneasiness of the bookcase parallels the insecurity you're feeling now that you're alone. The struggle to stay on top and not lose your balance symbolizes you fighting to regain control of your life. The emotions you feel as you imagine yourself standing on top of an unstable structure and the subsequent plummet to the ground will evoke emotions of fear, shame, and lack of control. These can all be used to color the monologue. Of course, I'm not recommending that you say the line "I stood alone on the beach" a certain way. Predetermining how you say a line limits you from discovering new moments. Rather, if your emotions bubble up and make you feel like you've lost control of your life, that will inherently color how you deliver the line. The underlying message here is that the memory techniques we're applying with the added level of emotionality to the stories will not only help you recall your lines, but also help you with your emotional approach to the piece.

Next, you should be looking straight ahead to the wall in front of you where the flat screen television is. The next line is "and watched the waves crash in the distance." Even though it's logical to picture yourself still on the beach after having jumped down from the bookcase, just to show how powerful your memory is, let's imagine that you're no longer on the beach. The net effect will be the same whether this part of the story is on the beach or not. In fact, it's important to point out that we're not creating a chain or link story where the associations of the images of the lines pegged to the Room Peg List objects need to be connected in any way. They can be linked or chained together at times if it makes sense, but the stories certainly can remain independent of each other. In this case, let's remove ourselves from the beach, even though the line is "and watched the waves crash in the distance."

Imagine that you're standing in the middle of the room and looking straight ahead at a beautiful sixty-inch LED 3-D flat screen television. Imagine you're wearing 3-D glasses and then you turn the television on. You instantly jump back as you see a fifty-foot wave come crashing out of the screen. You take the glasses off to see if it was real and realize that it's just the amazing picture on the television. You put the glasses back on and continue watching the waves in the distance. You can see every wave in great detail. The curve of the wave's wall. The white foam as it crashes. The sway from side to side. The bobbing up and down.

You feel sick to your stomach from watching the waves crash in the distance. You try to pull the 3-D glasses off, but they're stuck. The waves are building in height and speed. You can hear the crash of the waves getting closer. Your body is rocking back and forth, up and down. The waves continue to crash as they get closer and closer. You close your eyes to center yourself, and when you open them, a massive wave rushes straight out of the television screen and crashes on top of you. The room fills with water and you're tossed around under the waves. You kick and swim as hard as you can to get to the surface. You reach the top of the water and point the remote control at the television. You push the off button and as soon as the television goes dark, the waves disappear. You're left standing in the middle of your room, soaking wet and exhausted.

As you deliver your line, "and watched the waves crash in the distance," you can use the imagery of the waves consuming you and tossing you all around to help connect on a deeper level with the subtext and emotion of the monologue.

"Lightning danced across the night sky" is the next line of the monologue. You should now be looking at the far right corner in front of you where the Wurlitzer jukebox is located in your Room Peg List. Let's imagine that the jukebox is off. As you walk toward the unit, you reach into your pocket and take out a quarter. You slip the coin into the slot and the Wurlitzer comes to life. The neon lights glow, the tubes running top to bottom with water in them bubble, and the buttons where you select which record you want to listen to shine from within. You press the top right button, and the mechanical arm releases from its resting place, swings over to the stack of old records, plucks out the album, and drops it onto the turntable. The needle gently touches down onto the spinning record.

You hear a bit of crackling and then BAM!!!!! A massive lightning bolt shoots right out of the top of the jukebox. The electrical bang blows you off your feet and you go flying backward. You stand up and walk back to the jukebox and then BAM!!! Another lightning bolt blasts out of the top of the Wurlitzer, shoots straight up, and blows a massive hole through the ceiling. You look up and can see the night sky through the hole. You're captivated as the lightning dances across the sky in beat with the song. As the music begins to play louder, you hear the falsetto voice of Lou Christie singing his hit song "Lightnin' Strikes," and lightning continues to shoot out the top of the jukebox, illuminating the sky once again.

The lightning begins to change color from yellow to blue to red to orange to purple and back to yellow. You're amazed and feel alive, like electricity is flowing through your body. You tingle all over and feel goose bumps running down your arms. You place both hands on the jukebox and the vibration energizes you to your core. You hold on as you feel the energy building as the songs gets closer to the powerful chorus.

Then, BAM!!! Another bolt of lightning explodes and dances like a fast-flipping hip-hop dancer across the night sky. You look up and watch the amazing colors leap from left to right and back again.

The emotional undercurrent presented here is one of hope. The exhilaration you might feel as you relive this story when you deliver the line, "Lightning danced across the night sky," may help give the monologue more complexity. Instead of a single emotion of sadness playing throughout the entire piece, moments of hope or peacefulness will help turn the monologue into a dynamic performance. If your stories are all based in sadness, the monologue may come across as one note or flat. You may deliver a nice piece, but the more dynamic a monologue can be, emotionally speaking, the more effective it will be. Having different emotional moments throughout your monologue will create a stronger impact.

One note to help further clarify this technique and process. The memory techniques you're learning are to help you memorize your lines long before the performance takes place. We happen to be adding an emotional element to this specific monologue to demonstrate the dynamic nature of the technique, but it's critical to understand I'm not suggesting that during your performance you should be thinking about the association stories and pull yourself away, mentally, from the imaginary circumstances of the script. The memory techniques are being taught to help you get past the struggles most actors have with remembering their lines during the rehearsal process. Once the lines are memorized, you can get back to the Meisner, Strasberg, Adler, Hagen, etc. acting techniques you use to help develop your character, connect with the other actors, and deliver a powerful performance.

Over time, as you apply the memory principles, you'll easily remember your lines. Then you can push aside the association stories and simply deliver the lines while you're living truthfully in the moment as the character. Again, the memory techniques presented here are to help you during the rehearsal process and for the infrequent times when you do forget your lines during a performance. I point this out just in case you're asking yourself if during the performance you should be thinking about the moon playing the piano or the overstuffed couch covered in cats and dogs or the Wurlitzer shooting lightning. The answer is no. You should leverage these techniques during the rehearsal process, and then once your lines are memorized, you can leave the peg lists and stories behind.

Let's get back to the monologue. Your next line is "and I thought I could see heaven." Playing off of the feeling of hope we've established with the line before, let's create a story that somehow makes you believe you see your loved one at peace in heaven.

In your Room Peg List you should look to your right and see the large window. We must now peg the image of heaven to the window. I've used a window here instead of a piece of furniture to demonstrate that an empty wall or a corner with nothing in it can also be used. You'll see in a moment how the story will use the method of having the image of what we're trying to remember (heaven) crash through the wall—or window in this case—as the interaction with the Room Peg. Here we have a large window as our Room Peg, but a bare wall would be used the same way.

Imagine you're standing in the room at night. It's totally dark and there's a sense of calm all around. You look to your right and see the large window. It has three sections that are separated by beautifully carved wood molding. As you look at the window, you see a tiny beam of light form in the distance. You walk to the window and place both hands flat on the glass. It's cold to the touch, and a slight chill rushes down your spine. You move your face closer to the window to get a better look at the light, but your hot breath fogs the glass. You use your shirt sleeve to wipe the moisture from the window, and when the fog is gone, you see the beam of light has grown much brighter and is coming right toward you. The glow increases and the beam widens.

The bright light is pure white and illuminates the entire room. The intensity of the heat from the light increases and a feeling of warmness envelops you. You step back from the window and see that the glass has begun to heat up from the strong beam hitting it. Suddenly, the glass melts and drips to the floor. The beam of light wraps around you like a cocoon and lifts you off the ground. You look into the light and know it's a sign from heaven. You feel God's presence in the light. You are at peace. You feel loved. The light gently places you back down and unwraps itself from you. You watch as the light rushes back to the sky like a wave flowing back to the ocean. The beam grows smaller and smaller until it's just a tiny star flickering in the sky.

The peacefulness and the hope that is the emotional subtext here when you say, "and I thought I could see heaven," will once again help with developing different emotional levels in the monologue.

Your next line is a short one, "Max barked," but that doesn't mean you should overlook it or think that it doesn't have an emotional significance. Let's assume for a moment that the emotional journey you've created in the monologue so far has moved from shades of sadness to a form of hope. It might be an interesting acting choice to shake yourself awake and create a break from the deeper emotions by adding a lighter emotional layer to the monologue. Perhaps the dog barking scares you for a moment and brings you back to reality.

You should now be looking over your right shoulder to the back right corner at the wooden computer hutch from your Room Peg List. Imagine that you're walking toward the wooden computer hutch. It's a rustic wooden unit with two large cabinet doors that swing open like someone opening his arms for a big hug. The doors are closed and you need to get into the unit to turn on your computer. Just as you take another step toward the wooden computer hutch, both doors fly open and Max, your nine-year-old golden retriever, is standing and barking on top of your old computer monitor. You jump back in shock, and Max reaches out with both paws and pulls the wooden doors closed. Your heart skips a beat because you didn't know Max was inside the computer hutch, nor have you ever witnessed a dog open and close doors like that before.

You shake your head and realize you've tilted your head as you're looking at the computer hutch in the exact manner that Max tilts his head when he hears a strange noise. You take a gentle step forward toward the computer hutch, and just as your toe touches the ground, the doors swing open again and Max lets out a massive RRRUUUFFFF that blows your hair back. Max leaps off the monitor and tackles you to the ground. You roll around with Max for a few seconds and then he leaps off of you, jumps back inside the wooden computer hutch, uses his paws to grab both handles, and shuts the doors again.

Even though the line in the monologue is only two words, "Max barked," it does not mean it is without subtext. As every actor should know, even when there are no lines, there is always something going on subtextually. So a two word line definitely has meaning and should not just be thrown out there without creating a justification for it. Every word or phrase should be carefully analyzed when you're breaking down the script.

For our purposes of memorizing lines, the more images we have, the easier it will be to remember your lines. So turn as many words into images as possible to help you with the memorization process. As a reminder, just like the Number Peg Lists from the previous section, the items in your Room Peg List should never change. You'll need to create your own Room Peg List based on your own home, but this imaginary Room Peg List is a perfect sample to help you understand the process. As a note, when you build your own Room Peg List, it's best to pick a room in your home that has a lot of furniture or objects. Also, it should be a room that you're not planning on rearranging or redecorating anytime soon. The Room Peg List is most effective when the actual room remains exactly the same until you've locked your pegs into your mind. After that, you can rearrange your furniture and still go back to the original room in your mind.

In the back story we created for the monologue, let's imagine that one of your loved one's favorite activities was playing fetch with Max. Max always slobbered over the ratty old tennis balls he would retrieve, but your loved one never cared about the drool when she grabbed the ball from Max's mouth. The line, "and dropped a wet tennis ball at my feet," could have an emotional connection to this nostalgic game. It's not just a wet tennis ball. The wet tennis ball represents the loss of a loved one. It represents the loss of a companion.

Let's create a story for the images of the line that connects with our room peg. You should now be looking directly behind you on the back wall at the light panel with four switches. Let's imagine that this light panel is white and has dimmer sliders above the on-off buttons. Imagine the room is dark, so you turn around to walk to the light panel, but before you even take a step, you see the dimmer sliders start moving up and down on their own. You stop and stare at the light panel. All four dimmer sliders move down to their lowest position.

Then, suddenly, the one on the far right moves up and a wet tennis ball shoots out from the light panel and lands at your feet. The far right dimmer slider moves back down. You shake your head and rub your eyes. Then all four dimmer switches move up, and four wet tennis balls shoot out and land at your feet. The ratty old tennis balls are sopping wet, but not with water. They're covered in dog drool. You kick the tennis balls away with your left foot and one of the wet tennis balls gets stuck to your shoe. As you try to flick it off by using your other foot, the light panel begins machine gunning wet tennis balls at your feet. The wet tennis balls form a large pile around your feet, and you kick them away as fast as you can, but you can't keep up. The drool-saturated tennis balls stick to your feet, and you can no longer move. Then, just as quickly as it started, the light panel's dimmer switches slide down and stop shooting. You muscle your way out from the massive pile of wet tennis balls and kick at them until you're able to walk away.

So the overwhelming sensation of being repeatedly pelted with tennis balls is a stinging reminder of the loss of your loved one. How this makes you feel—perhaps like you're being buried alive—will color the delivery of your monologue.

You should now be looking at the floor in the middle of the room where your glass coffee table is placed. The glass coffee table is your ninth out of ten pegs in your Room Peg List. Your line is, "I sipped my coffee," so we must now create an association between the image of sipping coffee to the coffee table. Sometimes there are coincidences where the line you're trying to remember has an inherent connection to the peg itself. In this case, the sipping of the coffee and the glass coffee table work well together. The challenge is to not fall into the trap of creating a mundane story about sipping coffee and putting the cup down on the coffee table. Rather, despite the inherent connection, you must still create a compelling story that will be memorable.

Let's work back to the core emotion of sadness that we have chosen to emotionally prepare for before delivering the monologue in a performance or an audition. Imagine you're standing in the middle of the room directly in front of the glass coffee table. Suddenly, the clear table top grows dark and appears to be swirling around. It looks as if the glass has somehow turned into a liquid. The liquid top changes from a dark brown to a cream color, and the scent of hazelnut and coffee fills the air. You lean over, take a deep breath through your nose, and are amazed at the warm and comforting scent of a rich cup of coffee.

You dip your pinky finger into the liquid and feel the heat of the coffee that is somehow floating inside the coffee table. You put your finger in your mouth and taste the sweet hazelnut flavor. You kneel in front of the coffee table and lower your face toward the liquid. You put your lips on the surface of the coffee and sip. The flavor is deep and rich. The coffee warms your soul. You take a long sip, and as you swallow, your body begins to feel heavy. Your movements are sluggish and you can hardly find the energy to stand. You sink into the ground, lie under the glass coffee table, and look up at the hazelnut coffee floating above you. You reach up to touch the coffee, but your hand hits the glass and you can no longer touch or drink the coffee. The glass top slowly turns back to its clear form. The coffee is gone, and you lie on your back breathing deeply.

This feeling of slowing down and reaching out to touch something you desperately want to hold but can't will help bring the emotional level of the monologue back to the core emotion you've prepared for, a sadness or a longing for something lost.

In your imagination, you should now be standing in the middle of the Room Peg List. Your tenth peg is the four blade ceiling fan on the ceiling directly above you. Your line is "and dreamed of flying away." We must now turn the line into an image and peg it to the ceiling fan. Here again we have one of those fortunate situations where the image of the line "and dreamed of flying away" can be turned into something that associates perfectly with the four blade ceiling fan. However, just like the last peg with sipping coffee and the glass coffee table, we can't create a boring story of the ceiling fan blades simply flying away. Our association must be more powerful than logical. The story must have action and be anything but mundane in order for us to remember the line.

When you look up at the ceiling, you see the four blade ceiling fan and realize that it's spinning faster and faster. You feel the cold wind blowing and a chill runs down your spine. The blades pick up even more speed and you can hear the spinning like an airplane's propeller. The metal pole that holds the fan to the ceiling begins to wobble and pieces of the ceiling crack and fall down onto your head. The blades turn even faster and the screws holding the metal pole pop off and shoot out like bullets. The fan finally snaps free from the ceiling, but instead of plummeting down on top of you, it hovers just above your head like a helicopter.

The weight of the metal pole makes the blades rotate end over end, and as the metal pole swings past your head, you reach out and grab it. The blades continue to spin faster and faster. You extend your arms and point the pole toward the window. You bend your knees and leap off the ground. The ceiling fan in your hands shoots straight through the window, and as glass shards fly past your body, you burst through the window into the fresh air outside. You hold on tight as you fly higher and higher into the sky.

The act of breaking free from your surroundings mirrors the yearning in the monologue to disappear from the pain. The line "and dreamed of flying away" speaks of the desire to leave the pain behind and recapture a happier time before sadness overtook you. The feeling of holding onto the powerful ceiling fan as it pulls you out of your reality will help catapult you emotionally to that other place and time.

So there you have it. You've just finished the process of memorizing a monologue with the Room Peg List. To review, the first step was to create your Room Peg List by designating ten objects or locations in your room to act as the pegs in the room that you will associate the new information to. Step two was to break the monologue down into its images because we don't think in words, we think in pictures. Step three was to simply "peg" the image to the Room Peg List object in some memorable way. When you think about the Room Peg List object, you'll see the image of the line interacting with it, and the association story will help bring you back to the text you're trying to memorize.

Here is the monologue again:
The moon was full and the rain poured down like cats and dogs.
I stood alone on the beach and watched the waves crash in the distance.
Lightning danced across the night sky and I thought I could see heaven.
Max barked and dropped a wet tennis ball at my feet.
I sipped my coffee and dreamed of flying away.

Below in **bold** are the words that we turned into the images that were pegged to the Room Peg List.

The **moon was full** and the **rain poured down like cats and dogs**.
I **stood alone on the beach** and watched the **waves crash** in the distance.
**Lightning danced** across the night sky and I thought I could see **heaven**.
**Max barked** and **dropped a wet tennis ball** at my feet.
I **sipped my coffee** and **dreamed of flying away**.

Once you have your images identified in your monologue, the critical step is to create a meaningful, memorable, bizarre, crazy, insane, exciting, action-packed, impossible, emotional story of the image from the monologue interacting with your Room Peg List object or location.

There are two options regarding the linking of the emotion in the association story to the desired emotion of the monologue. In some cases it will help you connect to the emotional core of the monologue if your peg stories mirror the objectives, obstacles, actions, and emotions you're striving for as an actor when you perform the monologue. There may also be times when you feel it's more effective to ensure that your peg stories have no emotional connection to the monologue. In this second case, your objective is to strictly memorize the lines and get to the "acting" technique later.

Both versions work exceptionally well and you'll need to try each to determine which you feel more connected to. In the next section, we'll use the Journey Method to remember another monologue and we won't add any emotional connection from our peg stories to our monologue. It will strictly be a line memorization example.

It's time to take a break again. When you return, we'll review the monologue we just pegged to the Room Peg List to prove how quickly you can memorize your lines. After that we'll move on to The Journey Method. Close the book now and come back when you feel rested.

●●●●●●●●

Welcome back from your break. Remember, we take breaks because our minds recall information at the beginning and end of a learning session more than in the middle, so by taking frequent breaks, we increase our starts and stops and we retain more information. It's as simple as that.

Before we review the previous monologue, promise yourself that you won't look in the book for the line. As we progress through the review, if you stumble and can't recall the line, just move on. Sometimes when you take the pressure off and move onto the next peg in the room, the story or line you forgot before will jump into your mind. Make sure you have the paper that you drew with your room pegs. The paper you're holding should have the following pictures:

1. The back corner over your left shoulder **(UPRIGHT PIANO)**
2. The side wall as you look left **(OVERSTUFFED COUCH)**
3. The far left corner in front of you **(WOODEN BOOKCASE)**
4. The wall straight in front of you **(FLAT SCREEN TELEVISION)**
5. The far right corner in front of you **(WURLITZER JUKEBOX)**
6. The side wall as you look right **(LARGE WINDOW)**
7. The back corner over your right shoulder **(WOODEN COMPUTER HUTCH)**
8. The back wall behind you **(LIGHT PANEL WITH FOUR SWITCHES)**
9. The floor in the middle of the room **(GLASS COFFEE TABLE)**
10. The ceiling **(FOUR BLADE CEILING FAN)**

Let's begin. Stand up and hold this book in one hand and the Room Peg List paper in the other. Reread the ten locations and pegs, and as you do so, turn your head and your body in the direction of the next peg and imagine the object to be there. You need to lock these pegs into your mind. By connecting the peg to the location, you'll have a strong peg list to use for many years. Let's reread the list again now out loud:

1. The back corner over your left shoulder **(UPRIGHT PIANO)**
2. The side wall as you look left **(OVERSTUFFED COUCH)**
3. The far left corner in front of you **(WOODEN BOOKCASE)**
4. The wall straight in front of you **(FLAT SCREEN TELEVISION)**
5. The far right corner in front of you **(WURLITZER JUKEBOX)**
6. The side wall as you look right **(LARGE WINDOW)**
7. The back corner over your right shoulder **(WOODEN COMPUTER HUTCH)**
8. The back wall behind you **(LIGHT PANEL WITH FOUR SWITCHES)**
9. The floor in the middle of the room **(GLASS COFFEE TABLE)**
10. The ceiling **(FOUR BLADE CEILING FAN)**

Now that the pegs are becoming connected to the ten room locations, let's retell the story, one at a time.

Look to the back corner over your left shoulder and really see the upright piano. What is happening at the piano? Who is playing the piano? What do you see? Is it a person? No, it's a full moon. What does the moon look like? What song is the full moon playing? What colors do you see? How do you feel? What emotions are surfacing? Retell yourself the story.
What is the first line of the monologue?

_____

Now look to the left at the side wall. What is happening on the couch? Are people just sitting there? Do you see anything falling onto the couch? What is it? Do you see the cats and dogs pouring down onto the couch? What are the cats and dogs doing? Are they playing or fighting? Really tell yourself the story. What emotions dominate here?
What is the second line of the monologue?

_____

Look now to the far left corner in front of you where your wooden bookcase is. Describe the bookcase in detail. Is it new or old? Is it sturdy or flimsy? What is the wooden bookcase standing on? Is it a carpet or something else? Is it sand? Who is on top of the bookcase? Are you standing on the bookcase? Are you up there with perfect balance or are you teetering? Are you with anyone or are you alone? How do you feel? What emotions are you experiencing?
What is the third line of the monologue?

_____

Do you now see the flat screen television on the wall directly in front of you? Describe the television. Is it an old TV or is it one of those crystal clear 3-D televisions? What do you view in the television? Are you watching a show or do you see something else? What sounds do you hear? What do you feel, physically? Do you see the waves crashing? Are they close or off in the distance? What emotions do you feel?
What is the fourth line of the monologue?

_____

Look to the far right corner in front of you and see the Wurlitzer jukebox. Is it on or is it off? What color is it? Do you look at it from afar or do you move toward it? Do you put a quarter in the jukebox? What happens when it comes to life? What sounds do you hear? What colors do you see? What is moving inside the jukebox? What song is playing? Is it a slow song or an old rock-n-roll song? What happens when the chorus

starts? What shoots out the top of the jukebox? Is it smoke? No, it's a bolt of lightning. What color is the lightning as it shoots across the sky? Do you touch the lightning? How do you feel? What emotions run through you?
What is the fifth line of the monologue?

---

Look to your right now and see the large window. Are there drapes and blinds covering the window? Is it an ornate window? Do you see any trim? What colors do you see? Look through the window. What do you see in the darkness? Is there a light? What happens to the light? Does the light enter the room? What happens to the window from the heat of the light? Does the light touch you? How does the light make you feel? What does the light make you think of? Is the light as white as heaven? Do you feel afraid or at peace?
What is the sixth line of the monologue?

---

Turn your head and look to the back corner over your right shoulder where you've placed the wooden computer hutch. Describe the hutch in detail. What color is the wood? Is it old or new? How many cabinet doors are on the unit? Are they open or closed? Do you hear anything inside the wooden computer hutch? What happens next? Do the doors fly open? Who's inside? Is it an animal? Yes, it's a dog. What does he do? Does he stay in the wooden computer hutch or does he leap out at you? What do you feel?
What is the seventh line of the monologue?

---

When you turn directly behind you and look at the back wall, you should see the light panel with four light switches. What kind of switches are they? Are they the simple on-off/up-down switches or something different? Do you see dimmer sliders? What color are the dimmer switches? Is the room dark or light? Picture yourself walking toward the light panel. What happens to the dimmers? Do they stay in place or do they move up and down? Do you see anything come out from the light switch? What shoots out of the light switch? Is it a light or an object? Do you feel a wet tennis ball? Is it wet with water or something else? Does the wet tennis ball hit you in the chest or someplace else? Do you kick the wet tennis balls away?
What is the eighth line of the monologue?

---

Stand in the middle of the room and look at the glass coffee table on the floor in front of you. What do you see? Is the glass top see-through? Does the coffee table stay an inanimate piece of furniture or does it change? What changes do you see? Does the glass grow darker? What does it look like? Do you smell anything? What aroma is in the air? Do you just watch the glass coffee table change or do you do something? Do you touch anything? How does it feel? What temperature is it? What do you see? Do you taste anything? Do you remain standing or do you kneel down? What do you sip? Is it water or is it coffee? What flavor is the coffee? How does the coffee taste as you swallow? Where are you? How do you feel?

What is the ninth line of the monologue?

---

Look up to the ceiling to see the tenth peg in the room, the four blade ceiling fan. Is the fan off or are the blades spinning? How fast are the blades spinning? Do you feel air blowing down on you? Do the blades slow down or do they get faster? What do you hear? What do you see as you look up at the metal pole holding the fan to the ceiling? Does it seem stable or is it wobbling? What happens to the screws holding the fan? Does the fan break away from the ceiling? Does it fall and hit you or does it hover above you like a helicopter? How do you feel? Do you grab the pole? Does the fan stop spinning or does it get even faster? Do you remain on the ground or does the fan lift you off the ground? Where does the fan take you? Do you fly straight up or out through the window? What do you feel? What do you see?

What is the tenth line of the monologue?

---

In a moment, place this book down, but hold the paper with your drawing of the Room Peg List. Don't look at the drawing though. Just know it's there if you need it, but by now, the room pegs should be locked in your mind. Take a deep breath. Take another deep breath. As soon as you close this book, mentally walk through each peg and the association story silently. Take your time to recall all of the details of the stories. Then say each line of the monologue out loud. Put the book down now and run through it once more.

●●●●●●●●

How did you do? Did you get every line? Did you have any problems recalling the stories? If you had any challenges, as mentioned before, it's a result of you not fully connecting with the story. To make the line memorization process easier for you, you will need to create your own stories that are bizarre, intense, emotional, action-packed, and interesting to you.

Try it once again. Say the entire monologue now.

_____

_____

_____

_____

_____

_____

_____

_____

_____

_____

•••••••••

Here is the monologue so you can see just how well you did.

The moon was full and the rain poured down like cats and dogs.
I stood alone on the beach and watched the waves crash in the distance.
Lightning danced across the night sky and I thought I could see heaven.
Max barked and dropped a wet tennis ball at my feet.
I sipped my coffee and dreamed of flying away.

You now have the skills to take any monologue you're handed and begin the process of creatively remembering your lines. This is a wonderful tool to have in your arsenal when you're on an audition. How many times have you been handed sides or pages from a scene to memorize before walking in for an audition? How much more effective could you be if during the audition you spend all your time truly listening and responding to your audition partner as opposed to looking down to read the lines? How much more will you set yourself apart from the other actors auditioning if you're the only one who never needs to look down at the script?

Directors want to work with actors who will make their job easier and enjoyable. By demonstrating at the audition that you're a master at memorizing your lines, directors can trust that you'll bring that same level of professionalism to the production if they offer you the part. While your fellow actors are cramming and struggling to remember their lines before their audition, you can move quickly past the line memorization part of the process and focus on breaking down the script, figuring out what your objectives are, and developing character choices to help make your audition stand out.

To provide you with another important memorization tool, we'll move onto the Journey Method. But first, it's time to take another short break.

●●●●●●●●

# THE JOURNEY METHOD

The Journey Method builds upon the principles taught in the previous chapters, but instead of creating pegs that are images associated to numbers or objects in a room, your Journey Method pegs are physical locations along a journey from location A to location B. As an example, imagine you're at your house and need to go to the grocery store. What major locations would you pass along the journey as you drive to the grocery store? Let's create an imaginary set of ten locations that will act as your Journey Method location pegs for the next monologue.

## Journey Method Peg List

1. Your house
2. Soccer field
3. Theater
4. Post office
5. Pharmacy
6. High school
7. Fire station
8. Bank
9. Ice cream shop
10. Grocery store

It's time once again to draw. Take out a blank piece of paper and something to draw with. The more colorful you make it, the quicker you'll remember your list. We don't remember things that are mundane, so if your drawings are in pencil, you'll have a harder time remembering them than if you draw your Journey Method Pegs with colored pencils or markers.

Draw a map of this imaginary town we've created. Make sure to draw each building or location around the page in a logical path that you would drive past if you were really driving from your house to the grocery store. It's important that your drawing has the locations in sequence so when you take the mental journey, you'll be virtually driving past the buildings in a sequential order. We don't want you haphazardly driving north, then south, then east, then west. Rather, your route should be a logical progression from your house to the soccer field to the theater and so on. Your pegs must be in order.

After you draw your ten locations, draw a line around your town that shows the path you would drive to go from your house to the grocery store. If your instinct is to draw a road instead of just a line, you're on the right path in terms of making things interesting.

Now that the map of your town is created, let's continue. Above are your ten Journey Method Pegs. Just like the sun and the door were part of your Number-Rhyme Peg List and the upright piano and the large window were part of your Room Peg List, the ten locations we've created will be your Journey Method pegs. Of course, you'll need to create your own list of locations to make a real Journey Peg List for yourself, but for the purposes of this exercise, the list here will do just fine.

Also, you can have many Journey Peg Lists and they don't all have to be ten locations. Some may have only a few places and others can go on and on and on. In a moment you'll read your second monologue and begin the process of identifying the key images in the text and turning those images into stories that interact in a memorable way with the locations we've created as our Journey Method pegs. The process will be just like when you mentally looked around the room at your Room Pegs, but this time you'll take a mental journey from your house to the grocery store. As you virtually drive through town, you'll see your images interacting with the location pegs and that will lead to you remembering the lines of the monologue.

As you work through this exercise, you may find it helpful to physically walk around as if you were really driving the route from your home to the grocery store. Reinforcing the imagery through physical movement will add a kinesthetic layer to the process that will accelerate the memorization.

In this exercise, we'll take a different approach to the stories we create. Last time we added a sense of emotion to our stories to help us connect to the subtext and feeling of the piece as we rehearsed and performed it. In this exercise, we'll focus strictly on the line memorization and not add any emotional aspect to the story. You'd use this method if your objective were to simply memorize your lines so that afterwards you could begin the process of building your character without any predetermined feeling or way of performing the monologue. Both methods are valid and work equally well. You'll need to try different approaches to determine if you connect more to one than the other or if you're comfortable using both for different scripts.

Let's explore the next monologue. There's a religious text called *Pirkei Avot*, which in Hebrew means "Ethics of our Fathers." The resource is a collection of the ethical teachings and advice from historic leaders in the Jewish religion. Regardless of your religious affiliation, one verse in *Ethics of our Fathers* lends itself to become a concise and powerful monologue, so we'll use it in this exercise. The seventh passage in chapter five compares the attributes of a wise person to an unwise person.

Here is the text:

Seven things apply to an unwise person and seven to a wise person. A wise person does not speak before one who is greater than he in wisdom or years; he does not interrupt his fellow; he does not rush to respond; he asks relevant questions; he answers accurately; he discusses first things first and last things last; on what he did not hear, he says 'I did not hear;' and he admits to the truth. The opposite of these traits describes the unwise person.

It's a clever little piece that delivers a powerful message. For the purposes of turning this into a dramatic monologue, we'll add the line, "Which one are you?" to the end. Imagine you're auditioning to play a religious figure in a show and are asked to deliver your audition monologue as if it were a sermon. This piece would fit perfectly. The text itself has wonderful imagery, which is perfect for our purposes, and equally important, it delivers a message that really makes the audience think. If at the end of the monologue, the casting director is asking himself whether he was a wise or unwise person, you would have left a lasting impression, and that moves you one step closer to landing the role.

As before, we must now break the text into chunks that have strong imagery because our mind doesn't think in words, it thinks in pictures. Then we must "peg" the image of the text to our Journey Method Peg List with memorable stories. By now, this process should be enjoyable and much easier to do. Remember that this time we're attempting to memorize the lines without emotionality so that the words are simply raw text that flows out easily. Once you have the lines memorized, you can begin your work as an actor to figure out how to bring the monologue to life. Below you will find the passage broken down into ten lines.

1. Seven things apply to an unwise person and seven to a wise person.
2. A wise person does not speak before one who is greater than he in wisdom or years;
3. he does not interrupt his fellow;
4. he does not rush to respond;
5. he asks relevant questions;
6. he answers accurately;
7. he discusses first things first and last things last;
8. on what he did not hear, he says 'I did not hear;'
9. and he admits to the truth.
10. The opposite of these traits describes the unwise person. Which one are you?

Next, we must create strong images that represent the text and associate those images to the Journey Method Pegs. Here are the stories to help you memorize the monologue, but if the associations don't connect with you, then you should create your own. As mentioned before, when you create the stories yourself, they become more meaningful to you and that will translate into faster memorization and recollection.

**Journey Method Peg 1: Your House**
**Monologue Line 1: Seven things apply to an unwise person and seven to a wise person.**

Imagine you're standing outside your house looking at the front door. Suddenly, the door opens and two people walk out. First to exit is a punk of a student smoking a cigarette. He's eighteen years old, wears ripped, oil-stained jeans, a wrinkled t-shirt with the number seven on the front, a ball cap turned sideways, and has piercings of small metal posts through his nose and lips. As he walks out of the house, he kicks and crushes a pile of seven cardboard boxes onto the front lawn. Once all of the damaged boxes are on the grass, he walks behind them, applies a heavy coat of lighter fluid, strikes a match, drops the little flame onto the boxes, and watches them burn. He takes seven copies of his job application from his pants pocket, crumples them up, and throws them on the fire.

You look past the unwise person and see a distinguished gentleman exiting the house. You realize that the man is a professor dressed in a three-piece charcoal-colored suit. He's sixty years old, has a full head of gray hair, silver spectacles, and stands upright as he walks toward a podium on the driveway. Before he begins to speak, he reaches seven times into his bag of Wise brand low sodium baked potato chips and eats seven healthy and crispy snacks. He begins to speak of things a wise man would philosophize about, and you learn that he's giving a lecture on seven attributes of social demographics as he gestures to seven neatly placed wrapped boxes on a table. The boxes are arranged in size from smallest to largest as you move from right to left.

The imagery of the punk kid easily makes you think of an unwise person. The seven on his shirt and the seven boxes link you back to the text of seven things. The use of the word "applies" when talking about how he puts the lighter fluid on the boxes and the reference to the seven applications pulled from his pocket both link you to the word "apply" in the monologue. The imagery of the wise professor eating seven Wise brand potato chips before he delivers his lecture and the seven boxes he uses as his props link you to the second part of the line, "and seven to a wise person."

Say the line once more. "**Seven things apply to an unwise person and seven to a wise person.**" Now close your eyes, retell yourself the story of the unwise person and the wise person, then say the line again without looking at the book.
Line 1:_____

**Journey Method Peg 2: The Soccer Field**
**Monologue Line 2: A wise person does not speak before one who is greater than he in wisdom or years;**

Imagine that you drive away from your house, and as you head to the grocery store, the first location you pass along the way is the soccer field. (Trace the route with your finger on the map you drew. This tactile sensation is yet another element to connect you to your Journey Method Peg List). You stop your car to listen to the older referee deliver his pregame instructions to one of the teenage boys' teams. The name of the team is the Wizards. The Wizards' coach is standing at the end of the line next to his squad. The boys are rowdy, not showing the older referee respect, and talking before the referee can explain the rules. The coach screams at his team, "Hey, guys! Quiet down. The referee has been doing this for thirty years. He's much wiser than all of you combined and he knows more about the game than you ever will, so show some respect and don't speak before the referee talks to us." The older referee nods in appreciation to the coach for helping get the young men settled down. The referee walks back and forth in front of the players and checks their cleats, shin guards, and uniforms. He also makes sure no one is wearing jewelry. Once he's satisfied that the boys are ready physically, he begins his speech.

With a deep voice and booming English accent that sounds like he's stepped right out of a Shakespearean play, the older referee says, "A wise person does not speak before one who is greater than he in wisdom or years. I know you are all wise young men and will stay silent as you listen to me. Since I am smarter than you with respect to the rules of the game and because I am older than you, I know you will be respectful."

The goalkeeper at the end of the line interrupts the older referee and says, "Yo, ref," but before he can finish his question, all of the other players turn to the keeper and say, "Dude, shut up. A wise person doesn't speak before one who is greater than he in wisdom or years."

The keeper raises his hand, and the older referee says, "I have finished explaining the rules of the game and you now have a clear understanding of what I expect from you. Mr. Goalkeeper, what is your question?" The keeper says, "Um, can I go pee?" The team laughs, the coach shakes his head in embarrassment, and the older referee smiles and says, "Yes, you may."

As you drive away, you think to yourself that what the referee told the young men was a powerful life lesson. A wise person does not speak before one who is greater than he in wisdom or years. As you drive down the road, you hear the older referee blow his whistle to start the game.

If you weren't speaking the referee's lines out loud as you read them, please go back and say them out loud now. Make sure you speak with your best English accent so that you sound like you're in a Shakespearean play. Do that now and then come back to this section.

The act of speaking out loud and using the English accent helps make this story interesting. It adds color and excitement, and when we expand a mundane referee lecture into a theatrical performance, we help manufacture interest in the information we're trying to remember. This line of the monologue—"a wise person does not speak before one who is greater than he in wisdom or years"—delivers a powerful message. The immature boys need to learn this lesson and the imagery that we've created here between the older English referee and the players will help you remember the line.

Say the line once more now. "A wise person does not speak before one who is greater than he in wisdom or years." Place your finger back on your house on the map. Think about the story of the unwise and wise person and then say the first line of the monologue. After you say the first line, move your finger to the soccer field and retell yourself the referee story. After you retell the referee story, say the second line.

Now say the first and the second line one after the other.

Line 1:_____

Line 2:_____

## Journey Method Peg 3: The Theater
## Monologue Line 3: he does not interrupt his fellow;

As you continue driving, the next location you pass is the community theater. Imagine an old wooden playhouse with character and history. As you stop in front of the theater, you see there's a rehearsal taking place for an outdoor concert. The performer singing is an elderly and blind African-American man who's emotionally consumed with the lyrics of the hymn *Amazing Grace*. The piano player accompanying the performer is a young and talented teen. The blind old man sings, "Amazing Grace, how sweet the sound, that saved a wreck like me. I once was lost but now I'm found. Was blind, but now I see."

Upon hearing the lyrics sung incorrectly, the young piano player jumps from his bench and says, "Clarence, I'm sorry to interrupt you, old fellow, but you sang the wrong words. It's not 'wreck.' It's 'wretch.' And it's not 'I'm found,' it's 'am found.'"

With that, Clarence stomps his foot, slams the microphone stand into the floor, and screams, "Who is this fool that interrupts his fellow performer? A wise man does not interrupt his fellow. I demand a new pianist immediately."

The director and stage manager grab the young piano player by both arms and drag him off the outdoor stage and toss him onto the lawn. A young female pianist sits down at the piano and begins to play the introduction to the song. Clarence regains his composure, takes the microphone, and with deep emotion sings, "Amazing Grace, how sweet the sound, that saved a wretch like me. I once was lost but now am found. Was blind, but now I see."

Just as you should have reread the referee with an English accent as if you were in a Shakespearean play, you should have been singing *Amazing Grace* with feeling. If you didn't sing it, please go back now and reread this section and be sure to sing the song with all your heart and soul.

By adding the music to this line, we add yet another layer of memory technique to help you recall the monologue. Melody often triggers the recollection of text. How many times have you been in the car listening to the radio and a song comes on that you haven't heard for years, but as soon as the lyrics begin, you sing every line as if you were reading the words? The connection of words to music is powerful and in this case, we use the singing in the story to connect us to the line "he does not interrupt his fellow." Although this line from the monologue isn't sung, once you relive Clarence singing *Amazing Grace*, you'll very quickly recall him yelling to the young piano player, "A wise man does not interrupt his fellow."

Trace your finger back to your house on the map and start from the beginning of your journey. Retell yourself the story at your house and then say the first line. Retell yourself the story from the soccer field and then say the second line. Retell yourself the story at the theater and then say the third line.

Now say the first, second, and third lines one after the other.

Line 1:_____

Line 2:_____

Line 3:_____

**Journey Method Peg 4: The Post Office**
**Monologue Line 4: he does not rush to respond;**

Continue on the journey by moving your finger from the theater to the post office. As you stop in front of the post office, you see a long line outside of people holding packages and letters, waiting for their turn at the counter. People are getting frustrated with having to wait so long and the people in the back of the line start getting rowdy. People begin screaming, "What's the hold up?" and "What's taking so long?" Then, like some bizarre version of the children's game of telephone where one person whispers a sentence to the next person in line, a message from the front is shouted from one person to the next. The first man by the door screams, "The guy at the counter is as slow as mud. Someone asked him a question and he does not rush to respond."

An old woman with a walker says, "Huh? What did he say?" and a young mother holding her baby says to the old woman, "He said that the guy at the counter is as slow as mud. Someone asked him to get something and he does not rush to respond." The old woman says, "He does not rush to respond? Does he think we have all day to stand in line? I have Bingo in ten minutes. He'd better hurry up."

A bearded man a few people back waves his arms and says, "Hey! What's going on up there?" and a frustrated teen standing behind the old woman yells back, "The guy at the counter is as slow as mud. Someone asked him to ship a Bingo machine and he does not rush to respond."

People start shouting from the back, "What's going on?" Another woman in the middle of the line yells back, "The guy at the counter is as slow as mud. Someone said his machine is broken and that he does not rush to respond."

With that, a mob mentality forms and everyone starts to scream, "He does not rush to respond. He does not rush to respond. He does not rush to respond." Then all the people run to the main door, push their way inside to the lobby, and wave their letters and packages high in the air. You shake your head and are happy that you didn't have to go to the post office today.

As you visualize the scene at the post office, it's important that you make the story come to life by adding a lot of action, color, and excitement to the people in line. The more vivid and active you make the scene in your mind, the easier it will be to recall the information. Reread or retell yourself the story associated to the post office and really hear the different people say the line, "He does not rush to respond."

Now trace your finger back to your house on the map and start from the beginning of your journey. Retell yourself the story at your house and then say the first line. Retell yourself the story from the soccer field and then say the second line. Retell yourself the story at the theater and then say the third line. Retell yourself the story at the post office and then say the fourth line.

Now say the first, second, third, and fourth lines one after the other.

Line 1:_____

Line 2:_____

Line 3:_____

Line 4:_____

## Journey Method Peg 5: The Pharmacy
## Monologue Line 5: he asks relevant questions;

Once again, use your finger to trace the route on your map. Move from the post office to the pharmacy. As you drive toward the pharmacy (in your mind), you see a massive celebration taking place. It looks like a county fair or a carnival. There are rides, games, food trucks, clowns, and thousands of people walking around with cotton candy and balloons. There's a giant banner above the pharmacy that reads, "Congratulations, Mike! He Asks Relevant Questions!"

You're so intrigued that you park your car, get out, and walk to the crowd in the parking lot. When you arrive at the main stage, you see a team of pharmacists in white lab coats all throwing Mike the pharmacist up in the air in a celebration of some kind. The manager takes the microphone and says, "Today we honor Mike because he asks relevant questions. And because he asks relevant questions, Mike is being honored today as our Employee of the Year."

The crowd cheers for Mike. You move closer to the stage and continue to listen to the manager. He says, "Mike never just gives medication to the customer. He asks relevant questions to make sure that they're getting the right medication for their symptoms and he always makes sure the customer knows how much to take."

Some super enthusiastic woman screams out, "I love you, Mike. You ask relevant questions and you're my hero!" The crowd cheers. Mike stands at the front of the stage and like a rock star dives head-first into the crowd to start his body surfing adventure. Mike dives right toward you, so you put your arms above your head to support Mike's body. He lands in your hands and you buckle a little to support his weight. A few more hands reach up and pass Mike above everyone's head from the front of the crowd to the back.

While Mike is crowd surfing, everyone chants, "We love Mike. He asks relevant questions. We love Mike. He asks relevant questions. We love Mike. He asks relevant questions."

Even though you never met Mike, you're swept up in the pandemonium and join in the chanting of "We love Mike. He asks relevant questions." Once Mike is passed all the way around, he arrives back at the stage where he takes the microphone and delivers a very moving "thank you" speech. The crowd cheers again as you walk back to your car. As you drive away, you hear the sound of people still cheering, "We love Mike. He asks relevant questions."

This time, your involvement and active participation in the story will help you recall the line of the monologue, "He asks relevant questions." The more personal you make the story and the more you actually get involved in the story as opposed to just observing things happen, the more memorable it becomes. You can also see that prior to this we've use imagery of the line when needed or we've used the actual line. Both options are valid approaches to remembering the text. You'll need to discover for yourself which style helps you remember the line quicker. As you make this technique your own, you'll discover where your comfort zone is and develop skills you can repeat for fast line memorization.

Now, trace your finger back to your house on the map and start from the beginning of your journey. Retell yourself the story at your house and then say the first line. Retell yourself the story from the soccer field and then say the second line. Retell yourself the story at the theater and then say the third line. Retell yourself the story at the post office and then say the fourth line. Retell yourself the story at the pharmacy and then say the fifth line.

Now say the first, second, third, fourth, and fifth lines one after the other.

Line 1:_____

Line 2:_____

Line 3:_____

Line 4:_____

Line 5:_____

You may be questioning why we continue to go back to the beginning each time. It may appear as if we're slipping back into a pattern of rote memorization by sheer repetition; however, that is not the case. The purpose of forcing you to go back to the start of your journey after each line is to make you apply the process of retelling yourself the story before jumping ahead to try to recall the line. After you've circled through the retelling of the different stories at the different Journey Method locations multiple times, your ability to recall the details of the stories and the actual monologue lines themselves will accelerate.

As mentioned before, the objective here is not to remember this particular monologue about the wise and unwise person, but rather to train you in a process that helps you memorize your lines quickly and creatively and that can be applied to any script. You must relive the stories in order to get back to the lines. Forcing you back to your house each time will ingrain the technique in you so you'll be able to apply your new skills in your acting career.

We're now halfway through this exercise and it's time to take a short break, just to let your brain relax. If it's nice outside, take a short walk. Breathe in some fresh air before you come back to the book. If it's not nice outside, perhaps you could do a few pushups or stretches to wake up your body.

●●●●●●●●

Welcome back. Before we begin with the next five associations to our Journey Method Peg List, it's important to review the first five lines.

Put your finger on your house on the map and start from the beginning of your journey. Retell yourself the story at your house and then say the first line. Retell yourself the story from the soccer field and then say the second line. Retell yourself the story at the theater and then say the third line. Retell yourself the story at the post office and then say the fourth line. Retell yourself the story at the pharmacy and then say the fifth line.

Now say the first, second, third, fourth, and fifth lines one after the other.

Line 1:_____

Line 2:_____

Line 3:_____

Line 4:_____

Line 5:_____

I hope the monologue is coming to you easily now. If you're struggling with recalling the lines, it's because the stories didn't mean enough to you. If that's the case, go back to the lines you're having problems with and expand or change the stories to something more meaningful and memorable to your way of thinking. It's extremely important that you personalize this as much as possible, as soon as possible. Let's move on to the next five lines.

## Journey Method Peg 6: The High School
## Monologue Line 6: he answers accurately;

As you pass the high school, you see a long line of students driving their cars into the school parking lot. The first thing that catches your eye is that all of the cars are Acuras. You see black Acuras, white Acuras, silver Acuras, and yellow Acuras. The parking lot policeman checks to make sure that each student has a parking pass before he allows them to proceed. You see the officer stop one student and make him get out of his car. You pull over and stop your car to watch the interaction between the officer and the student. The policeman tells the young man that because he doesn't have a parking pass, he needs to stand next to his car and answer a few questions. The student nervously complies. The officer says, "I'm going to ask you a series of questions and if you answer accurately, you may park your car. Do you understand?" The student nods his head yes.

Horns honk from the long line of kids trying to park their cars so they're not late for school. You hear kids shouting from their cars things like, "Let's go," "Come on dude, just let him park. You're gonna make us all late," and "Just get on with the questions, he'll answer them accurately!" The officer asks the kid for his name, student ID number, address, phone number, guidance counselor's name, and the name of all his teachers in order of his class schedule.

Horns continue to honk and the student is getting more nervous by the minute. The officer says, "If you answer accurately, you may park. If not, you need to go home." The student takes a deep breath and answers accurately. He gets every question right. The policeman picks up his bullhorn and makes an announcement. "He answers accurately."

With that, all the students in line cheer, honk their horns, and whistle. The kid gets back into his car and drives forward to the parking lot. A few more cars drive past the policeman until he stops a yellow Acura. The policeman makes another announcement on his bullhorn. He says, "I have another student with no parking pass. You know the drill. If he answers accurately, he may pass." You again hear a series of horns honking and students screaming. You turn your car back on and laugh as you drive away.

Here we used two images to connect us with the line "he answers accurately." The Acura car will make you think of the word "accurately" and the words spoken by the policeman are the actual line of the monologue. This dual approach will help strengthen and accelerate the recollection of the words.

As you read these stories, it's critical that you begin veering off on your own, using your imagination, and make the stories meaningful to you. Since no two people think exactly alike, it's impossible for one story to connect to everyone in exactly the same way. By now you should have a firm grasp on the technique, so if the silly stories written here don't spark your interest and make you easily recall the monologue, it's time for you to either expand the story or replace it with something you prefer. Have fun with this process and don't judge yourself or your thoughts. Allow yourself the freedom and permission to let your imagination run wild. The crazier your story, the farther away from boring it will be, and our brain remembers things that are unusual, strange, and bizarre.

Now, trace your finger back to your house on the map and start from the beginning of your journey. Retell yourself the story at your house and then say the first line. Retell yourself the story from the soccer field and then say the second line. Retell yourself the story at the theater and then say the third line. Retell yourself the story at the post office and then say the fourth line. Retell yourself the story at the pharmacy and then say the fifth line. Retell yourself the story at the high school and then say the sixth line.

Now say the first, second, third, fourth, fifth, and sixth lines one after the other.

Line 1:_____

Line 2:_____

Line 3:_____

Line 4:_____

Line 5:_____

Line 6:_____

## Journey Method Peg 7: The Fire Station
**Monologue Line 7: he discusses first things first and last things last;**

As you continue on your journey, you stop at the next light and to your left is the fire station. The building has two large garage doors to help fire trucks and ambulances pull out of the building quickly. As you wait at the light, you see firefighters and paramedics running through an emergency drill to help train rookies on proper procedure when they're out on a call. The first drill you watch is a gurney race to see how fast the rookies can get a patient off the ground, strapped into the gurney, and into the ambulance. You see two dummies lying on the ground on one side of the parking lot and on the other side are two rookies standing behind gurneys. The chief blows his whistle and the two young paramedics push the gurneys across the parking lot. The rookie on the right arrives first and gets the dummy strapped onto the board. The second young paramedic arrives moments later and straps his dummy onto the board but makes mistakes in his strapping technique and has to restart the process. The first rookie raises his hand to notify he's ready for assistance in lifting the patient onto the gurney. One of the veteran paramedics runs over and helps lift the board onto the gurney. Once on the gurney, the first rookie secures additional straps and pushes the patient back to the ambulance. He looks over his shoulder to see the last rookie has caught up and is now running fast behind him. As the first rookie arrives at the ambulance, he positions the gurney perfectly into the ambulance. The gurney's legs fold beneath the patient and it slides into place. He closes the ambulance door and the chief blows the whistle. The chief says, "No discussion needed. First place goes to rookie number one and last place goes to rookie number two." All of the veteran paramedics laugh and clap for the rookies' efforts.

The story could stop there if you can connect the images back to the line "he discusses first things first and last things last." But if you need additional imagery to help recall the line, simply create your own story. The more you take ownership of this process, the faster you'll master this technique and the faster you'll be able to apply it to your lines. The result will be you "off-book" faster than ever before.

Now, trace your finger back to your house on the map and start from the beginning of your journey. Retell yourself the story at your house and then say the first line. Retell yourself the story from the soccer field and then say the second line. Retell yourself the story at the theater and then say the third line. Retell yourself the story at the post office and then say the fourth line. Retell yourself the story at the pharmacy and then say the fifth line. Retell yourself the story at the high school and then say the sixth line. Retell yourself the story at the fire station and then say the seventh line.

Now say the first, second, third, fourth, fifth, sixth, and seventh lines one after the other.

Line 1: _____

Line 2: _____

Line 3: _____

Line 4: _____

Line 5: _____

Line 6: _____

Line 7: _____

## Journey Method Peg 8: The Bank
**Monologue Line 8: on what he did not hear, he says 'I did not hear;'**

As the light turns green, you drive past the fire station, pull into the bank parking lot, and enter the drive-through lane. You roll down your window and reach out to pull the plastic container from the air tube that pushes and pulls the money to and from your car. The old and rusty loudspeaker crackles. You hear static and what sounds like someone speaking, but you can't understand what the person is saying. It sounds like garbled gibberish. You yell from your car, "What? I did not hear what you said. Can you repeat that? I did not hear what you said."

The static comes again and this time it sounds like the teller is saying, "Wel....place....moment...." and then static blares again. You stick your head out the window and put your mouth close to the old speaker and shout, "I DID NOT HEAR. I SAID I DID NOT HEAR. PLEASE SAY IT AGAIN."

A third time, noise comes through the speaker and you can't make out anything the teller is saying. You turn your car off, grab your deposit, jump out of your car, and walk into the bank. You push your way past a few people and head straight to the counter. You see the drive-through teller sitting at her window and you scream, "Hey! Drive-Through Teller. Turn around."

An old woman turns around and looks at you. She's a wrinkled grandmother with a frail body. She slowly gets up from her chair and walks over to you. Suddenly you feel really guilty about yelling at this old woman. You put your head down and apologetically say, "Forgive me, ma'am. I couldn't hear you so I said I did not hear. I'm sorry I yelled at you." The old woman smiles and says, "That's okay, sonny. Sometimes people can't help being abusive, inconsiderate, and unwise. What I said was 'Welcome to Bank Wise. Please place your deposit in the container and I'll have you out of here in just a moment.' But since you did not hear me, why don't you take your sorry butt out of my bank now and get back in your car. You're holding up the line."

With that, you turn and run out of the bank, jump in your car, put the plastic container back in the tube without your deposit, and drive away. You're totally embarrassed and disgusted by how you treated the old woman.

The line of the monologue is "on what he did not hear, he says 'I did not hear.'" The interaction between you and the bank teller should bring you quickly back to the line. The more vivid you make the action of you screaming at the teller through the rusty speaker, the more interesting the story becomes. And the more interested you become in the story, the faster you'll be able to recall the line.

As before, you'll now go back to the beginning and retell the story starting from the house. You may feel inclined to rush through the story and jump ahead to this new line, but try to slow things down and force yourself to retell the details of each story. It's through the stories that you'll ingrain the monologue into your memory. If you rush through, you'll eventually lose details that make the association memorable. That, in turn, could lead to you not being able to recall the line. Take your time and remind yourself of your objective. It's not to remember this particular monologue. Rather, your objective should be to learn and master a new skill that you can apply to all monologues and dialogues going forward. So don't rush through the process. Enjoy it and retell yourself every detail of the story.

Now trace your finger back to your house on the map and start from the beginning of your journey. Retell yourself the story at your house and then say the first line. Retell yourself the story from the soccer field and then say the second line. Retell yourself the story at the theater and then say the third line. Retell yourself the story at the post office and then say the fourth line. Retell yourself the story at the pharmacy and then say the fifth line. Retell yourself the story at the high school and then say the sixth line. Retell yourself the story at the fire station and then say the seventh line. Retell yourself the story at the bank and then say the eighth line.

Now say the first, second, third, fourth, fifth, sixth, seventh, and eighth lines one after the other.

Line 1:_____

Line 2:_____

Line 3:_____

Line 4:_____

Line 5:_____

Line 6:_____

Line 7:_____

Line 8:_____

## Journey Method Peg 9: The Ice Cream Shop
## Monologue Line 9: and he admits to the truth.

As you turn the corner toward the grocery store, you see mass hysteria outside the ice cream shop. There's a man on the ground being treated by a paramedic with what appears to be an insulin pump, there's a woman clutching her stomach as she screams in pain, and there's a mother hysterically crying as she injects her daughter with an epinephrine pen. In the middle of this commotion is a teenage boy who works at the ice cream shop and the mob is pushing and shoving him as he tries to fend them off with his ice cream scooper. You hear the crowd shouting things like, "Admit to the truth. Just admit that you didn't give the diabetic the sugar free ice cream. Come on and admit to the truth."

You hear another person yell, "Yeah! Admit to the truth. You served the woman who's lactose intolerant the real ice cream instead of the dairy free kind. Just admit to the truth." Then you hear the mother of the young girl scream at the top of her lungs, "Admit to the truth. You gave my daughter ice cream with peanuts in it after I told you she had a peanut allergy. Just admit to the truth."

You see the mob close in on the young ice cream scooper boy, and he finally breaks down and starts to cry. As he sobs, he says, "Yes, I admit to the truth. I did it all. I gave the diabetic sugar-filled ice cream. I gave the lactose intolerant woman ice cream with milk and I gave the little girl ice cream with peanuts in it. I'm so sorry. I admit to the truth. I should be fired."

The crowd chants, "Yeah. Fire him. Fire him. Fire him." Finally, the diabetic stands up, the lactose intolerant woman lets go of her belly, and the allergic little girl starts to skip around. Everyone is going to be just fine. The three people approach the ice cream boy, embrace him in a loving hug, and say, "We forgive you because you admitted to the truth." The ice cream shop manager comes outside and yells, "Since he admitted to the truth, I'm celebrating by giving everyone free ice cream."

And with that, the entire mob rushes back into the ice cream shop to get their free dessert. As you drive on toward the grocery store, you see the last person walk inside the ice cream shop and you hear the little bell above the door jingle.

The more vivid and manic you can make the mob scene, the stronger the images will be in your mind and the faster you'll get back to the line "and he admits to the truth." Remember that in this exercise we're not adding emotionality to enhance the performance of the monologue. Rather, any emotion that's created is simply to help you connect to the imagery and ultimately the line you're trying to remember. As proven in the Room Peg List monologue, you can add emotionality to the stories that could carry over into the performance of the piece. Alternatively, like we're doing here, you can simply use the stories as a vehicle to speed up the line memorization process independent of your emotional interpretation of the monologue.

As we've done before, now trace your finger back to your house on the map and start from the beginning of your journey. Retell yourself the story at your house and then say the first line. Retell yourself the story from the soccer field and then say the second line. Retell yourself the story at the theater and then say the third line. Retell yourself the story at the post office and then say the fourth line. Retell yourself the story at the pharmacy and then say the fifth line. Retell yourself the story at the high school and then say the sixth line. Retell yourself the story at the fire station and then say the seventh line. Retell yourself the story at the bank and then say the eighth line. Retell yourself the story at the ice cream shop and then say the ninth line.

Now say the first, second, third, fourth, fifth, sixth, seventh, eighth, and ninth lines one after the other.

Line 1:_____

Line 2:_____

Line 3:_____

Line 4:_____

Line 5:_____

Line 6:_____

Line 7:_____

Line 8:_____

Line 9:_____

### Journey Method Peg 10: The Grocery Store
### Monologue Line 10: The opposite of these traits describes the unwise person. Which one are you?

You finally arrive at the grocery store. As you pull into the parking lot, you see the most amazing thing. There's a teenager wearing a grocery store apron with the nametag "Reckless" on it. He has collected all the carts and assembled them into a long train. Reckless is standing on top of the carts, as if he's surfing, as they roll away from the grocery store. As he rides the carts around the parking lot, you hear him scream, "Which one are you? Which one are you? Which one are you?"

People in the parking lot jump out of the way to avoid being hit by the cart surfer. They gather in the front of the grocery store to watch this very unwise person engage in an extremely dangerous act. The surfer does tricks on top of the carts where he turns his body in the opposite direction that the carts are rolling. He does a handstand so his feet are opposite where they should be. He lies down on his stomach and then flips in the opposite direction onto his back. He jumps up in the air and lands inside the first cart of the train.

The store manager screams at the unwise employee, "Reckless. That is unwise behavior! It is the exact opposite of how you were trained. You are an unwise person and you will most certainly be fired for this. Are you a wise person or an unwise person?"

With that, Reckless jumps back on top of the carts, takes his employee apron off, and waves it above his head as he screams, "I'm an unwise person, but which one are you? Which one are you? Which one are you?"

The carts suddenly crash into a parked SUV and Reckless flies through the air and lands in the bushes. The manager runs over to make sure Reckless is okay, and after he sees Reckless laughing, the manager takes the apron and says, "You are unwise. I, on the other hand, am a wise person and that's why I'm glad to say that you're fired."

As the manager walks away, he shakes his head in disbelief as he repeats the question, "Which one are you?"

A few key images in this story are meant to make you think of the cart surfer as an unwise person. The name Reckless should paint a picture of an unwise person. Layer on top of that his insane action of cart surfing through the parking lot and there should be no question in your mind that he represents an unwise person. As you visualize him saying "Which one are you?" it's important to speak those words out loud. This will reinforce the imagery. When Reckless physically moves around the carts and shifts his body position in opposite directions multiple times, that is a key indicator that the word "opposite" is part of the line "The opposite of these traits describes the unwise person" that you're trying to remember.

For the final time, trace your finger back to your house on the map and start from the beginning of your journey. Retell yourself the story at your house and then say the first line. Retell yourself the story from the soccer field and then say the second line. Retell yourself the story at the theater and then say the third line. Retell yourself the story at the post office and then say the fourth line. Retell yourself the story at the pharmacy and then say the fifth line. Retell yourself the story at the high school and then say the sixth line. Retell yourself the story at the fire station and then say the seventh line. Retell yourself the story at the bank and then say the eighth line. Retell yourself the story at the ice cream shop and then say the ninth line. Retell yourself the story at the grocery store and then say the tenth line.

Now say all ten lines one after the other.

Line 1:_____

Line 2:_____

Line 3:_____

Line 4:_____

Line 5:_____

Line 6:_____

Line 7:_____

Line 8:_____

Line 9:_____

Line 10:_____

On the next page, you'll find the monologue so you can check to see how well you did. As mentioned before, if you struggle with any of the lines, it's because the stories didn't connect strongly enough with you. To fix this gap, you must go back and expand or alter the stories to make them bizarre and interesting for your way of thinking. Perhaps you need to make the stories more violent or maybe you need to paint them all pink and have fluffy bunny rabbits hopping around.

As you develop your style of creating these association stories, you must find your comfort and your un-comfort zones, then create your stories mainly in your un-comfort zone. Remember, we recall things that are out of the ordinary. If it helps you to remember your monologue faster by creating stories that you know are inappropriate or disgusting, just go with it. Allow your actor's imaginative instincts to guide you along your memory improvement journey.

Turn the page to read the seventh passage of chapter five from the religious text *Pirkei Avot* (Ethics of our Fathers*)*, the collection of the ethical teachings and advice from historic leaders in the Jewish religion that we've turned into a concise and powerful monologue comparing the attributes of a wise person to an unwise person.

1. Seven things apply to an unwise person and seven to a wise person.
2. A wise person does not speak before one who is greater than he in wisdom or years;
3. he does not interrupt his fellow;
4. he does not rush to respond;
5. he asks relevant questions;
6. he answers accurately;
7. he discusses first things first and last things last;
8. on what he did not hear, he says 'I did not hear;'
9. and he admits to the truth.
10. The opposite of these traits describes the unwise person. Which one are you?

Now that you know the lines of this monologue, you can make character choices, break down the script, determine who you are, where you are, why you're giving the speech, who your audience is, what you hope to accomplish, what your obstacles are, how you feel about the message you're delivering, and everything else that goes into creating a polished monologue ready for an audition or a performance.

It's time to take another break before we move onto the next monologue. Go ahead and spend some time relaxing away from the memory training.

●●●●●●●●

# THE BODY PEG LIST

It's important to restate what typically happens when an actor forgets his lines. Usually, it's not because he can't remember the specific words that come next. Rather, he can't recall the next thought or topic in the script. Once he hears the first few words of the line or is given a clue as to the general topic of the next section of the script, the light bulb turns on and the words come flowing back.

Think about times when you've forgotten what comes next and call "Line?" Once you hear the first few words of the next section read by someone offstage, aren't you amazed at how quickly you're able to continue saying your lines? All you needed was a trigger to help you reconnect with the next image or though in the script.

Let's move on to the Body Peg List and use the premise above along with the association skills you've learned thus far to quickly memorize another monologue. The Body Peg List is another example of how anything can be turned into a peg list to help you remember whatever you need to. This list of ten places on your body (technically, nine on your body and one just above it) will become your Body Peg List.

It's critical that you learn these body parts in their correct order and by the names provided here. The locations have very specific names because this list is actually the foundation for an advanced technique of turning numbers into letters through the phonetic alphabet, which is the basis for helping people remember any series of numbers. You can learn more about memorizing numbers (often called The Major System) through my website at www.jaredkelner.com or by researching the suggested material at the end of the book.

Let's apply the kinesthetic aspect of learning. Please stand up. Hold the book in one hand, and as you read the list of locations on your body out loud, tap that body part with your other hand. While we're going through this exercise, recognize that usually the inability to remember your lines is not about you failing to remember the actual words of the monologue, but rather it's a disassociation with the next thought in the monologue. In this section, we'll focus on the main thoughts of the monologue rather than breaking it down word by word or line by line, and by touching the various parts of our body during the learning process, we'll further ingrain the images.

As you read the Body Peg List you should say out loud, "Number one is Toes" and touch your toes as you say it. Then you would say, "Number two is Knees" and touch your knees as you say it, and so on.

# The Body Peg List

1. Toes
2. Knees
3. Muscle (This is your thigh muscle. Be sure to call it the muscle and not the thigh.)
4. Rear
5. Lungs
6. Shoulders
7. Collarbone
8. Face
9. Brain
10. Ceiling

Building on the concept that it's not the words themselves that actors struggle with remembering, the upcoming monologue and association stories will focus less on remembering every single word and focus more on the concepts or thoughts. As before, the steps remain the same. After you read the monologue, you then need to convert the piece into a series of images. Recall that we think in pictures, not in words, so the faster you get to the images that represent the words, the faster you can memorize the lines.

After you have created your images that represent the words, you then must "peg" or associate those images to something that you already know. That way, when you go back to the place you already know (the Body Peg List in this case), the new information you're trying to remember will be there and will be easily recalled. Here is the next monologue.

## The Art of Sales

The art of sales is a topic that has been studied for many years, and it is generally agreed that there are three attributes to a successful salesperson. The first is that they build solid relationships with their customers and their coworkers. The second is that they demonstrate that they are an expert in their field. They know their products and services and their competitors' products and services better than anyone else. Third, and probably most important, they always look for the win-win and never try to take advantage of their customers. If you follow these three principles—build solid relationships, demonstrate that you are an expert in your field, and always look for the win-win—then you will likely ride that rainbow to the proverbial pot of gold. But if you don't, if you just look for a quick sale, you may make some money in the short term, but you will not have longevity in sales. You'll just be a flash in the pan. So why am I telling you this now? Well, we are at the beginning of our fiscal year and we have a very large financial mountain to climb. And if we continue to do the same thing again and again, over and over without changing our approach, we will be spinning our wheels. That's one definition of insanity by the way, to do the same thing again and again and expect different results. But if you do follow these three principles—build solid relationships, demonstrate that you are an expert in your field, and always look for the win-win—I will be proud to shake your hand at next year's sales conference as balloons and confetti fall down on you as you walk across the stage as the best salesperson of the year. Now let's get out there and sell.

As you read the monologue above, did it make you think of any list previously presented in this book? If yes, turn the page to see if you connected to the images embedded in the monologue. If not, please reread the monologue now and see if you can discover what's coming next. Turn the page to find out more.

If you thought about the original Benchmark Challenge list of images, you're correct. The list below contains images from different sections of the monologue.

## Benchmark Challenge List

1. The Mona Lisa
2. "For Sale" sign
3. Brick building
4. The Nobel Prize
5. Two boxers with arms raised
6. Rainbow
7. Frying pan
8. Mountain
9. Hamster wheel
10. Confetti

Let's break it down together. Below is the monologue and in **(parenthesis)** you'll find the image from the list that represents the words.

## The Art of Sales

The art **(The Mona Lisa)** of sales **("For Sale" sign)** is a topic that has been studied for many years and it is generally agreed that there are three attributes to a successful salesperson. The first is that they build solid relationships **(Brick building)** with their customers and their coworkers. The second is that they demonstrate that they are an expert in their field **(The Nobel Prize)**. They know their products and services and their competitors' products and services better than anyone else. Third, and probably most important, they always look for the win-win **(Two boxers with arms raised)** and never try to take advantage of their customers. If you follow these three principles—build solid relationships, demonstrate that you are an expert in your field, and always look for the win-win—then you will likely ride that rainbow **(Rainbow)** to the proverbial pot of gold. But if you don't, if you just look for a quick sale, you may make some money in the short term, but you will not have longevity in sales. You'll just be a flash in the pan **(Frying pan)**. So why am I telling you this now? Well, we are at the beginning of our fiscal year and we have a very large financial mountain to climb **(Mountain)**. And if we continue to do the same thing again and again, over and over without changing our approach, we will be spinning our wheels **(Hamster wheel)**. That's one definition of insanity by the way, to do the same thing again and again and expect different results. But if you do follow these three principles—build solid relationships, demonstrate that you are an expert in your field, and always look for the win-win—I will be proud to shake your hand at next year's

100

sales conference as balloons and confetti **(Confetti)** fall down on you as you walk across the stage as the best salesperson of the year. Now let's get out there and sell.

Now that we have turned the words into images, we must "peg" the images to our Body Peg List, so when we go back to the thing that we already know (the places on our body), the new information (the Mona Lisa list) will be there. Then, to remember the lines from the monologue, simply start at your toes and retell yourself the association story to trigger the image that represents the next thought in the script. You'll very quickly recall the words. The process doesn't change. The only thing that is changing is the peg list itself.

As a reminder, the purpose of this book is to teach you proven memory techniques that leverage your inherent imaginative essence as an actor to accelerate the line memorization process, not to create character choices or a polished performance piece. It's important to remember that your job as an actor is to live truthfully, creatively, and instinctively under the imaginary circumstances of the playwright. To do that you must get past the line memorization part of the process so you can spend the majority of your rehearsal time working on the many aspects that go into creating a character.

Let's create our stories now. We must peg the following items to the Body Peg List:

1. The Mona Lisa must be pegged in some creative way to your toes.
2. "For Sale" sign must be pegged in some creative way to your knees.
3. Brick building must be pegged in some creative way to your muscle.
4. The Nobel Prize must be pegged in some creative way to your rear.
5. Two boxers with arms raised must be pegged in some creative way to your lungs.
6. Rainbow must be pegged in some creative way to your shoulders.
7. Frying pan must be pegged in some creative way to your collarbone.
8. Mountain must be pegged in some creative way to your face.
9. Hamster wheel must be pegged in some creative way to your brain.
10. Confetti must be pegged in some creative way to the ceiling.

### The Mona Lisa must be pegged in some creative way to your toes.

Imagine you're sitting in your chair in front of a blank canvas and all around you are painting supplies. You reach down and take off your shoes and socks. Then you place different sized paint brushes in between all of your toes. You dip each brush into a different color. You lean back in your chair, grab both sides of the seat with your hands, and lift your legs in the air. You paint a portrait of a woman and it's amazing. The face is simple yet beautiful, and she looks like she could be alive. You sit back as your toes cramp and you reach down and take the brushes in your hand. You lean forward to observe your masterpiece and realize that you just painted a perfect copy of the Mona Lisa by Leonardo da Vinci. Suddenly, the woman in the painting blinks and turns her head. You're frozen in disbelief. Then, the Mona Lisa speaks and says, "Are you Leonardo da Vinci?" You sit back, full of pride, and say, "No, I'm Leonardo da Toesy."

Certainly, this could never happen, and that's the point. Our mind remembers things that are crazy. As you retell yourself this story, try to really feel the brushes between your toes. Move your legs as if you were actually painting to add the kinesthetic aspect to ingrain the image. If this story doesn't work for you, then create a story that pegs the Mona Lisa to your toes in some wacky, insane way that's meaningful to you. If the story above works for you, then move on to the next body peg.

### "For Sale" sign must be pegged in some creative way to your knees.

Reach both hands down and feel the tissue just under your kneecaps. Imagine digging your fingers under your kneecaps and ripping them off. (Just imagine it, don't actually do it). Ouch. Did you hear the crack of the bone? Do you feel the blood running down your leg? Imagine two leg bones popping out from the hole where your kneecaps were and at the end of each leg bone a rusty metal For Sale sign appears and swings from left to right. You can hear the metal sign squeaking. The sign says *Broken Kneecaps: $1 each.*

Obviously, this story is violent and gross, but that makes it stand out. No one has ever really pulled his kneecaps off on purpose, so the insanity of it all makes it interesting, and our brain remembers things that we're interested in.

### Brick building must be pegged in some creative way to your muscle.

Stand up and flex your right thigh muscle. Now flex your left thigh muscle. Now go back to your right thigh muscle and flex it harder this time. Imagine that your muscle turns into bricks. Solid bricks, one after the other, form out of your right thigh muscle, and the bricks grow and grow until they become a brick building. You balance that massive brick building on your right thigh muscle as you flex your left thigh muscle hard, and the same thing happens on the left side. A single brick appears, then many bricks appear, and then the bricks grow into another massive brick building. You're standing with two brick buildings coming out of your two thigh muscles, and you feel the weight of them pushing you down, but you balance them and don't fall.

102

As you go through this story, imagine the feeling of the weight of the brick buildings and how you'd be pushed off balance trying to stand with the buildings jutting out from your legs.

## The Nobel Prize must be pegged in some creative way to your rear

Imagine you're on a stage in front of a very large crowd and you're receiving the Nobel Prize for the most amazing rear in the world. Around the globe, millions of people voted online and the masses agreed that your rear was so unique and so special that you should be awarded the Nobel Prize. As you stand on the stage and accept your award, you turn your rear toward the audience and give it a little shake. The crowd erupts in cheers. You take the Nobel Prize that's hanging at the end of a cloth necklace and you wrap it around your waist so the prize is dangling right in front of your rear. You give it a twirl and the crowd applauds again. You grab your rear and take a bow.

Have fun with this one. The lunacy of this story makes it memorable. Expand this with as many details as you can think of. What are all the amazing attributes of your rear that helped you win the Nobel Prize? Really revel in the craziness of this story and you'll never forget the Nobel Prize when you think of your rear.

## Two boxers with arms raised must be pegged in some creative way to your lungs

Put your hands on your chest and take a deep breath. Fill your lungs with air and hold it for a moment. Now exhale. Keep your hands on your chest and breathe again. Feel your lungs inflate and get hot. Imagine that your lungs throb and you feel the heat coming from inside your body. Suddenly, your lungs push hard against your insides and then you feel your skin tear. A red mass comes out the right side of your chest. Just after that, a yellow mass pushes out the left side of your chest. Your lungs are growing and coming out of your body. Then you notice that what you thought were your lungs are actually something completely different. The red and yellow masses look like boxing gloves. As the boxing gloves push out from inside your chest, you grab the red boxing glove in your right hand and the yellow boxing glove in your left hand and you pull them outward. You feel a hand inside each glove and see arms now coming from where your lungs used to be. You pull both gloves out and raise the boxers' arms above your head.

This story is a bit twisted. The physical sensation of the boxing gloves coming through your skin and the act of pulling the boxers' arms out may cause you to wince a little. Those uncomfortable feelings will help you remember two boxers with arms raised when you think of your lungs. The more you get into the details and sensations of the stories, the more interest you will create in them. The higher the interest, the faster you will remember the lines; it's that simple.

### Rainbow must be pegged in some creative way to your shoulders.

Imagine that your right shoulder starts to tingle. It's the same sensation you get when your arm falls asleep. The tingling slowly turns into a tickle, which makes you giggle. You look over at your right shoulder and see that it's glowing red, orange, yellow, green, blue, indigo, and violet. Then, magically, a tiny rainbow begins to grow right out of your shoulder. You look above you as the rainbow arcs and comes to rest on your left shoulder. You feel the heat of the rainbow on both shoulders and above your head. You look at your left shoulder and a tiny pot of gold appears. It's a small cast iron pot with little gold coins. Then you look to your right shoulder and you see a small leprechaun climbing up the rainbow. You watch as he pulls himself to the top, then rides the rainbow down and splashes into the pot of gold. He laughs as he throws his treasure up in the air.

Now we're back to a cute, feel-good story. It helps to break up the types of association stories you create so that they don't all have the same feeling. This variation will make each association more interesting. Once again, though, if the stories presented here don't interest you, you must create your own.

### Frying pan must be pegged in some creative way to your collarbone.

Think of the saying "Hot Under the Collar." Feel the heat coming from your collarbone. It should feel stinging hot like sizzling oil. Feel your collarbone with your right hand. Imagine wrapping your fingers around your collarbone and pulling it out. Feel the weight of the bone as you pull. Suddenly the collarbone turns into a hot cast iron frying pan full of popping and sizzling oil. Feel the sting of the hot oil as it jumps out of the pan and lands on your collar. Look in the frying pan and see the little pieces of collarbone that are frying in the hot oil. Put the frying pan down onto the stove and carefully pick the pieces of your collarbone out of the oil. Reassemble your collarbone one piece at a time. Push the hot fried collarbone pieces back into your neck and feel the bones pop back into place.

This is bizarre for sure, but the sensation of physical pain in your collarbone and the imagery of the pieces in the frying pan help make this story memorable. It's scary. No one enjoys that kind of pain, so the fear factor helps turn this story into something you're compelled to remember.

### Mountain must be pegged in some creative way to your face.

Most people who are just starting to apply these memory techniques will look to the literal or the obvious when first trying to create their stories. In this case, many people will immediately think of two associations when trying to peg a mountain to their faces. They may think of Mount Rushmore and imagine their face on the mountain. Or they may think of their big nose as a mountain.

Either of these can work, but they can't be passive. Just like the acting concept that "Acting is Doing," the association stories must be bursting with action in order to make them memorable. If you imagine your face on Mount Rushmore next to the other presidents, you must be doing something, not just be carved there as an inanimate object in stone. And you can't just be talking to the other presidents. Acting is not about talking, and these memory techniques follow the same principle. If all you're doing in your association story is talking, then the story won't have enough action or craziness to trigger a memory that will link you back to the line you're trying to memorize. You must always be doing something active in your stories, and talking is the farthest thing from actively doing. Perhaps your face is carved in between Theodore Roosevelt and Abraham Lincoln and you start blowing kisses to the right and to the left. Maybe you try to bite President Lincoln's beard or perhaps you try to lick President Roosevelt's mustache. What would happen if that caused Presidents Washington and Jefferson to turn their heads and spit rocks at you? Do you feel your face being pelted with tiny boulders from the Black Hills of South Dakota?

The other story that people tend to think of is their nose growing into a mountain. This one could be a lot of fun if you keep adding onto it. Imagine that you feel your nose swell, and then suddenly your nose splits open and a giant mountain erupts from your face. It grows so high that the snow-capped tips poke through the clouds. You see many ledges and cliffs with goats walking on trails. You see people hiking, rock climbing, and rappelling off the mountain. The goats leap off the cliffs and land on your face. The rock climbers lose their grips and plummet into your face. The rappellers descend and land in your eyes. Keep expanding on this story. But you must remember that the Body Peg is the face and not the nose, and you must make the story bursting with action.

As mentioned before, the Body Peg List leverages the phonetic alphabet process to convert numbers to letters and the number eight must be linked to the "F" sound, so you must remember the peg is the face, not the nose. (To learn more about turning numbers into letters, please visit www.jaredkelner.com and look for the ten-hour audio program or perform an Internet search on The Major System or the Phonetic Number System).

The second point to remember is that the stories must always include plenty of action. Think of these stories as an improvisation exercise you might have in an acting class. Pretend the teacher says, "Create a scene where your face turns into a mountain." What would you do? How would you create that in front of your acting class? The more you allow your imagination to run wild and free, the faster you'll master these memory techniques. If the two suggestions above don't connect with you, then create your own story that pegs your face to a mountain.

## Hamster wheel must be pegged in some creative way to your brain

Imagine that screwed into the top of your head is a rusty old hamster wheel and standing inside it is a cute little hamster. You're sitting on the couch and have no energy. Your mind is blank and you feel like a zombie. The hamster starts to run and the wheel spins faster and faster. As the wheel turns around and around, your energy level increases and you feel your brain turn on like an engine in a racecar. You feel the neurons firing in your brain and you jump to your feet.

The hamster keeps running and the wheel spins even faster. Your brain begins to throb and you feel a deep headache forming inside your skull. You reach up to stop the wheel, but the hamster bites your finger. The hamster runs and the wheel spins so fast that suddenly sparks shoot from your brain as the metal wheel scrapes against your skull. Your hair catches on fire. Your brain is pounding. You run over to the sink and turn on the faucet. You stick your head under the water and you hear the hiss as the fire goes out and the wheel stops spinning. You stand up as water drips down your head and onto your face. The hamster shakes himself dry and begins to walk at a normal pace. You feel your brain function normally and your headache goes away.

As with previous stories, it's sometimes easy to fall into the trap of being too simple, so it's critical to take the story to a place that's bizarre. If this story was only about a hamster running in a wheel to make your brain work, it would have been funny but not packed with enough action to make it memorable. If there wasn't enough action, you'd get to the brain on your Body Peg List and you'd think to yourself, "There's something on my head, but I can't remember what it is or what it's doing." It's the crazy action of the speedy hamster, the fire, the headache, and the water that pack the story full of action. Action makes the story memorable.

## Confetti must be pegged in some creative way to the ceiling.

Imagine you look up at the ceiling and the plain white paint begins to sparkle like there's glitter forming from within. The white color glows as little sections turn to yellow, red, blue, purple, green, orange, pink, and a myriad of other colors. Then you see tiny objects sprinkling down from the ceiling. It starts like a light drizzle, and you see beautiful pieces of colorful confetti floating down. One piece of metallic green confetti hits you right in the corner of your eye and you blink and use your pinky finger to scoop it out.

As you tilt your head back, you get a mouthful of paper confetti. You spit it out and feel a few pieces of confetti stuck in between your teeth. You look back up and the white ceiling is gone and in its place is a kaleidoscope of colorful confetti pouring down on you. The confetti piles up at your feet, and before you have time to react, you realize you're buried up to your waist in confetti. You're stuck and try to dig out, but more and more confetti falls down from the ceiling. You look up at the ceiling and feel the confetti beat down on top of you. Within seconds, you're buried up to your neck, and you take one last breath before you become completely submerged in the confetti.

Then suddenly, it all stops. The confetti stops pouring down. You hear something that sounds like a vacuum and you see that the ceiling has begun to suck the confetti back up inside itself. All of the confetti that had fallen down now shoots back up into the ceiling. Little by little your body becomes free as the confetti shoots upward. After a few minutes, you're completely free, and you dust off the last pieces of confetti from your shirt and shake the confetti from your hair. You look back up at the ceiling and see the colorful sections return to white. You look around the room and there's no confetti anywhere. The ceiling is perfectly white and normal as if nothing happened.

In an acting exercise known as the Coffee Cup exercise, during your normal morning coffee time you're asked to become in tune with the coffee. Really feel the weight and heat of the cup in your hands. Really feel the heat of the coffee as you sip it. Really taste the flavor of the hot liquid. Really feel the sensation in your throat as you swallow. Then, after you pay attention to your coffee for many mornings, in class you attempt to recreate the physical sensations without the coffee cup. It's a process to challenge your imagination and tie your memory to your senses.

To make this story about the confetti real for you, you can go through a similar process as with the coffee cup. Really imagine what it feels like to have a little piece of metallic confetti hit you in the corner of your eye. Really imagine the taste of a mouthful of paper confetti. Really imagine picking the confetti out of your teeth. The more real you make the physical sensations, the more memorable the story becomes. And when you really believe the story, then you'll very quickly be able to recall the confetti when you think of the ceiling. When you think of the confetti, that will trigger the recollection of the lines, "I will be proud to shake your hand at next year's sales conference as balloons and confetti fall down on you as you walk across the stage as the best sales person of the year. Now let's get out there and sell."

Before we run through the exercise to recall the Body Peg List, the list of ten images, and the lines of the speech, it's important to point out again that for this section, we're focused more on the concept of recalling the next major thought as opposed to remembering the individual words. Of course, memorizing the script word for word will be critical at some point soon, but this exercise is presented to prove the theory that when actors get stuck on certain lines, it's not because they can't remember the actual words, it's because they can't recall the next thought in the script. And once they're prompted with the next concept or thought or image, the lines flow back to them quickly.

Let's take this one step at a time by first recalling the ten Body Peg List locations. It may help if you stand up and touch the parts of your body as you run through this list.

1. What is the first Body Peg List location?
2. What is the second Body Peg List location?
3. What is the third Body Peg List location?
4. What is the fourth Body Peg List location?
5. What is the fifth Body Peg List location?
6. What is the sixth Body Peg List location?
7. What is the seventh Body Peg List location?
8. What is the eighth Body Peg List location?
9. What is the ninth Body Peg List location?
10. What is the tenth Body Peg List location?

Turn the page to see if you were right.

## The Body Peg List

1. Toes
2. Knees
3. Muscle (This is your thigh muscle. Be sure to call it the muscle and not the thigh.)
4. Rear
5. Lungs
6. Shoulders
7. Collarbone
8. Face
9. Brain
10. Ceiling

Now let's go through each peg and retell the story to see if you can recall the list we pegged to the Body Peg List.

1. What were you doing with your toes? Retell the story in detail.
   Now what is the first item on the list you're trying to remember?
2. What were you doing with your knees? Retell the story in detail.
   Now what is the second item on the list you're trying to remember?
3. What were you doing with your muscle? Retell the story in detail.
   Now what is the third item on the list you're trying to remember?
4. What were you doing with your rear? Retell the story in detail.
   Now what is the fourth item on the list you're trying to remember?
5. What were you doing with your lungs? Retell the story in detail.
   Now what is the fifth item on the list you're trying to remember?
6. What were you doing with your shoulders? Retell the story in detail.
   Now what is the sixth item on the list you're trying to remember?
7. What were you doing with your collarbone? Retell the story in detail.
   Now what is the seventh item on the list you are trying to remember?
8. What were you doing with your face? Retell the story in detail.
   Now what is the eighth item on the list you're trying to remember?
9. What were you doing with your brain? Retell the story in detail.
   Now what is the ninth item on the list you're trying to remember?
10. What were you doing with the ceiling? Retell the story in detail.
    Now what is the tenth item on the list you're trying to remember?

Here is the list of ten things you're trying to remember. If you missed any of them, it's only because you didn't connect with the story presented earlier and you should take the time to expand or modify the story to make it your own. The more the stories come from your imagination, the faster you'll remember the information. Here is the list.

1. The Mona Lisa
2. "For Sale" sign
3. Brick building
4. The Nobel Prize
5. Two boxers with arms raised
6. Rainbow
7. Frying pan
8. Mountain
9. Hamster wheel
10. Confetti

Reread the monologue one more time. As you get to each section that ties back to the Body Peg List and the associated images, physically touch the specified part of your body.

# The Art of Sales

The art **(The Mona Lisa - touch your toes)** of sales **("For Sale" sign - touch your knees)** is a topic that has been studied for many years, and it is generally agreed that there are three attributes to a successful salesperson. The first is that they build solid relationships **(Brick building - touch your muscle)** with their customers and their coworkers. The second is that they demonstrate that they are an expert in their field **(The Nobel Prize - touch your rear)**. They know their products and services and their competitors' products and services better than anyone else. Third, and probably most important, they always look for the win-win **(Two boxers with arms raised - touch your lungs)** and never try to take advantage of their customers. If you follow these three principles—build solid relationships, demonstrate that you are an expert in your field, and always look for the win-win—then you will likely ride that rainbow **(Rainbow - touch your shoulders)** to the proverbial pot of gold. But if you don't, if you just look for a quick sale, you may make some money in the short term, but you will not have longevity in sales. You'll just be a flash in the pan **(Frying pan - touch your collarbone)**. So why am I telling you this now? Well, we are at the beginning of our fiscal year and we have a very large financial mountain to climb **(Mountain - touch your face)**. And if we continue to do the same thing again and again, over and over without changing our approach, we will be spinning our wheels **(Hamster wheel - touch your brain)**. That's one definition of insanity by the way, to do the same thing

110

again and again and expect different results. But if you do follow these three principles—build solid relationships, demonstrate that you are an expert in your field, and always look for the win-win—I will be proud to shake your hand at next year's sales conference as balloons and confetti **(Confetti - point to the ceiling)** fall down on you as you walk across the stage as the best salesperson of the year. Now let's get out there and sell.

Put this book down and try to deliver the monologue by simply working your way up from your toes. Take your time. Really relive the stories to the fullest extent. Don't rush through the process to jump ahead to the script. Keep reminding yourself that you're learning a memorization technique, not specifically trying to memorize this specific monologue to use as an audition piece. The monologue presented here is just a tool to help you apply the memory principles. That's why it's important to work through the process and master it as best you can, so when you actually do apply the technique to a real monologue you're working on, you'll start with a solid foundation. Put the book down now and deliver the speech.

Welcome back. I hope you were able to apply the power of the Body Peg List to help you recall The Art of Sales speech. As you noticed, there's a section that repeats, when you say the three attributes of a successful salesperson for a second time before getting to the rainbow section. Did you find yourself physically touching your muscle, your rear, and your lungs a second time? If you did, then you're really connecting to the kinesthetic aspect of the memorization process. The Body Peg List is a powerful tool and the more you use it, the faster you'll master the technique.

In the next section, we move on to applying memory techniques and peg lists to remembering dialogues, but before we start that section, it's time to take another break.

●●●●●●●●

# SECTION 4:
# MEMORIZING DIALOGUES

Unfortunately, most actors rely on uncreative methods for memorizing their dialogue. Does this sound familiar? You highlight your lines and use a piece of paper to cover them, then read the other character's line as you try to remember your own. You then move the paper down to reveal your line. If you got it right, you slide the paper down to the next set of lines. If you got it wrong, you re-cover your line and try again.

Although this process of pounding the lines into your brain will work over time, it's in direct conflict with the creative and imaginative thought processes of an actor. Rather than continue with rote memorization, the memory techniques presented here take advantage of the actor's natural creative abilities to accelerate the memorization process.

Imagine that you're at an audition and the Director or Stage Manager hands you sides with some dialogue on it. If you could apply the memory techniques presented here, you'll get "off-book" fast so during your audition, you can put all your focus and attention onto the other actor, connect with them and live truthfully in the moment.

In this section, we'll explore two imagination-based processes for memorizing dialogues by using the Animal Peg List and the Number-Association Peg List.

## THE ANIMAL PEG LIST

For the first dialogue, we'll use the Animal Peg List. Just like the Room Peg List and the Journey Method where you went on a mental trip around a room and from one location to the next around town, the Animal Peg List is a mental journey through a zoo. In the Animal Peg List, we create an imaginary zoo where the animals live in habitats one after the other and the animals in these habitats are in alphabetical order. Each animal in the zoo represents the next letter of the alphabet. For the letter "A" we have alligators in the first habitat. For the letter "B" we have bats in the second habitat. For the letter "C" we have cats in the third habitat. For the letter "D" we have dogs in the fourth habitat. And so on. Here is my suggestion for the animals in the Animal Peg List; however, if you'd prefer to change the animals to something more meaningful to you that would be fine. If you'd rather see antelope instead of alligators or cows instead of cats, then by all means change the animals. The only rule is that the spelling of the animal must start with the correct letter in the alphabet.

As a side note, some memory experts use the Animal Peg List and the journey through the zoo to help remember a deck of playing cards. There are fifty-two cards in a deck and twenty-six letters in the alphabet (half the number of cards). By going through the zoo twice and "pegging" the image of the card to the animals, you can remember the order of a deck of cards. Perhaps the first trip through the zoo all the animals are male and the second time they're all female. Or the first time the animals are all colored white and the second time the animals are multicolored.

The challenge of memorizing the order of a deck of cards is an excellent way to practice the association techniques. To do this you would need to create images of each playing card that make you think of the card. Perhaps for the King of Hearts you would turn the card into an image of Brad Pitt or Robert Redford or any handsome and romantic male actor. Maybe the Jack of Clubs is Jack Nicklaus, the champion golfer. Perhaps the Six of Diamonds is a beautiful ring with a six carat diamond. Then you would "peg" the image of the card to the animals in alphabetical order. Again, this challenge is an excellent way to work out the imagination muscle and help you master the memorization techniques.

Here are the animals of the Animal Peg List that I suggest you use:

| | |
|---|---|
| A: Alligator | N: Newt |
| B: Bat | O: Octopus |
| C: Cat | P: Penguin |
| D: Dog | Q: Quail |
| E: Elephant | R: Rat |
| F: Flamingo | S: Snake |
| G: Giraffe | T: Tiger |
| H: Hyena | U: Unicorn |
| I: Iguana | V: Vulture |
| J: Jellyfish | W: Walrus |
| K: Kangaroo | X: Xenops |
| L: Lion | Y: Yak |
| M: Monkey | Z: Zebra |

Below is the short script that will be used for this exercise:

**John:** What time is the party over?
**Mary:** Midnight.
**John:** Are you drinking tonight?
**Mary:** No. I'm the designated driver.
**John:** What present did you buy them?
**Mary:** A blender.
**John:** Do you need me to wrap it?
**Mary:** Yes and put a bow on it.

This is a short script, but it will work perfectly to demonstrate how to apply the Animal Peg List. The first step is to turn the lines into images and then associate the images in some crazy way to the animals in alphabetical order. If the stories presented below don't spark your interest, then expand or replace them to make them your own. It's critical that the association stories are wacky, bizarre, unbelievable, and emotional for your way of thinking. Also, remember that action in your stories is a vital element to the process.

### The first animal in the Animal Peg List: Alligator
### John's line: What time is the party over?

Turn the line above into the image of a wristwatch wearing a party hat whose hands are spinning around and around so much that the watch itself is turning over and over. Then associate this watch to the alligator. Imagine that you're walking through the zoo and you come to the first habitat and you crack up because you see an alligator wearing a party hat trying to walk, but he keeps turning over and over and looks like he's totally drunk. He has wristwatches on all four legs and the watches are wearing pointed cone party hats. The dial hands on the watches are spinning around and around, and that is causing the alligator to slip, fall, and roll over again and again.

### The second animal in the Animal Peg List: Bat
### Mary's line: Midnight.

Turn the line above into the image of a grandfather clock turning exactly to midnight and you hear it chime with twelve deep gongs. Now associate this image to the bat. Imagine you walk to the next habitat and see a dark and gloomy environment. You feel a chill down your spine as you walk closer. Instead of animals roaming around, you see hundreds of grandfather clocks, but they're all hanging upside down from the branches of trees and from the ceiling of a cave. Suddenly you hear a thunderous gong. Then another gong. And another. Eleven gongs and then one more. Just as the twelfth gong sounds to signal midnight, the doors of every grandfather clock open and out of the clocks' bellies a million bats fly out. The sky grows dark as the bats block out the moonlight. You scream and run away.

**The third animal in the Animal Peg List: Cat**
**John's line: Are you drinking tonight?**
    As you approach the next habitat, you see an elegant cocktail party taking place, but all of the guests are cats. There are thousands of cats all dressed in sophisticated aristocrat outfits. They're holding martini glasses and conversing in pompous accents. They sound like they've just arrived from some high society country club. But the only thing that every single cat is saying is, "Are you drinking tonight?" Over and over you hear different cats say, "Are you drinking tonight?" "Are you drinking tonight?" "Are you drinking tonight?" And each time, the other cat holds up its martini glass, nods its head, takes a large gulp of vodka, and smiles.

**The fourth animal in the Animal Peg List: Dog**
**Mary's line: No. I'm the designated driver.**
    Right next to the cat habitat is the dog habitat. As you walk toward the dogs, you see the cats have all jumped up onto the ledge between the two habitats and continue asking the question "Are you drinking tonight?" but this time they're asking the dogs. As you get closer to the dog's habitat, you see many dogs sitting in a group of chairs that are set up in a circle. There's a sign above the dogs that reads Alcoholics Anonymous. The dogs are all dressed in chauffeur uniforms, complete with the hats.
    One at a time, each dog stands up to tell its story. The first dog says, "Hi, my name is Rufus and I am an alcoholic. I have been sober for three years now and no, I will not drink with the cats because I'm the designated driver." The next dog says, "Hi, my name is Fido and I am an alcoholic. I have been sober for six years now and no, I will not drink with the cats because I'm the designated driver."
    The cats continue to call over to the dogs and taunt them with their martinis. Suddenly all of the dogs bark at the cats. The dogs leap from their chairs and jump up onto the wall between the two habitats. The cats retreat in fear, dropping their martini glasses to the ground as they scatter. The dogs all stand proud on top of the wall and say, "No. I'm the designated driver."

**The fifth animal in the Animal Peg List: Elephant**
**John's line: What present did you buy them?**
    You move on to the next habitat to see the elephants. Turn the line above into the image of an elephant balancing on a big red ball like they do in the circus. The elephant is rolling on the ball and juggling five boxes of

presents all wrapped in beautiful colors. As he balances on the ball and juggles, he rolls over to a large vending machine that has more presents inside. The elephant uses his trunk to pick up a dollar bill from the ground. He inserts the dollar bill into the vending machine and buys another present. The new present comes out of the vending machine and the elephant picks it up with his trunk and adds it to his juggling. He repeats the process three more times, buying different size presents and adding them to his balancing and juggling routine.

### The sixth animal in the Animal Peg List: Flamingo
### Mary's line: A blender.

To your left, you hear a loud grinding sound so you rush over to the next habitat and you're nauseated by what you see. You scream in horror as you watch the massacre of innocent flamingos. There's one giant flamingo wearing full rebel military attire and he's leading his army in the capture and murder of innocent flamingos that wouldn't join his regime. One by one the captured flamingos are tossed into a giant blender. Once the blender is full of flamingos, the rebel leader puts a black rubber cap on top of the glass container and stomps on the button labeled "Purify." The flamingos inside are immediately ground up and turn into a frothy pink liquid. You gag as you watch this heinous crime.

(One comment about this tragic story. This is cruel and disgusting, but the image of flamingos getting blended into a pink liquid is so strong that you won't forget the line "A blender" when you think about visiting the flamingo habitat in the zoo. Sometimes violent images are the most powerful ones to help you remember your lines.)

### The seventh animal in the Animal Peg List: Giraffe
### John's line: Do you need me to wrap it?

Let's use the image of the word "wrap" in two ways:  to wrap as in to wrap a present and to rap as in to sing a rap song. Both versions will help bring you back to the line, "Do you need me to wrap it?"

Imagine that as you walk toward the giraffe habitat you hear a rap song playing over a loudspeaker. You feel the thumping of the bass notes reverberate inside your chest. As you approach the giraffes, you see a concert stage with multicolored lights and smoke flowing out from two smoke machines. On stage are three giraffe rappers wearing their baggy jeans so low you can see their underwear. They have gold chains around their necks, baseball caps turned sideways, and dark sunglasses. They're rapping a song called "Do you need me to wrap it?"

As they jump around the stage rapping, they also pull out rolls of wrapping paper. When they get to the chorus of the song and rap the words, "Do you need me to wrap it?" they wrap the wrapping paper around their long necks. By the time the rap song is over, the three giraffes have wrapping paper all up and down their necks. They take a bow and strut offstage.

**The eighth animal in the Animal Peg List: Hyena**
**Mary's line: Yes and put a bow on it.**
  You turn and walk toward the last habitat that is open and see a beautiful hyena with flowing blonde hair sitting at her makeup table brushing her hair. She's wearing an elegant silver gown and seems to be dressing for a party. She puts her hairbrush down and picks up a black bow from the table. She ties the bow around some hair from the left side of her head. Then she picks up a red bow and ties the bow around some hair from the right side of her head. She looks at herself in the mirror and says, "Yes." She picks up a blue bow and ties up some more hair. Then she ties a green bow, a gold bow, and a purple bow. She looks at herself and screams, "YES." The hyena is getting so excited by the way she looks in all her hair bows that she laughs in pure delight. She's in ecstasy with the bows in her hair. Finally, she composes herself, stands up from her makeup table, and heads out to her party.

  Now it's time to go back to the beginning of the zoo and relive the stories associated with the animals in the Animal Peg List. Remember that the objective is not to simply memorize the short script presented here, but to master a memory technique that you can apply to plays and scenes you're actually working on. With that in mind, be sure not to rush through, simply so you can say John's or Mary's lines. Make sure you're taking the time to first say the animal from the peg list, then retell yourself the story, then finally say the line.

**The first animal in the Animal Peg List:** _____
**John's line:** _____

**The second animal in the Animal Peg List:** _____
**Mary's line:** _____

**The third animal in the Animal Peg List:** _____
**John's line:** _____

**The fourth animal in the Animal Peg List:** _____
**Mary's line:** _____

**The fifth animal in the Animal Peg List:** _____
**John's line:** _____

**The sixth animal in the Animal Peg List:** _____

**Mary's line:** _____

**The seventh animal in the Animal Peg List:** _____

**John's line:** _____

**The eighth animal in the Animal Peg List:** _____

**Mary's line:** _____

Turn the page to see if you were successful in applying the Animal Peg List to recall this dialogue.

Here is the script again so you can see how well you did.

**John:** What time is the party over?
**Mary:** Midnight.
**John:** Are you drinking tonight?
**Mary:** No. I'm the designated driver.
**John:** What present did you buy them?
**Mary:** A blender.
**John:** Do you need me to wrap it?
**Mary:** Yes and put a bow on it.

As you can see, by turning the lines into images and then pegging those images to the next animal on the list, you can very easily remember any length script. If you have more than twenty-six lines and you wish to use the Animal Peg List, you have a few options. You can create multiple stories with the images of your lines, peg them in sequence to one animal, and then move onto the next animal for your next set of lines. By pegging multiple lines to one animal, you're able to keep an entire thought in one location before moving to the next animal and next thought in the script. Another option is to peg one thought to one animal as we did above, move onto the next animal for the next thought, and take multiple trips through the zoo. Each time through, you'd add a specific attribute to the animals or to the stories. For example, the first time through may have all male animals, then the second time the animals would all be female. The third time every animal could be black and the fourth time every animal could be white. The fifth time every animal could be encased in a block of ice and the sixth time every animal could be on fire. By adding an attribute that stays with the group of twenty-six animals, you can very easily keep the stories from overlapping or getting jumbled. Before you move on to the second exercise for remembering dialogues, why don't you take a short break?

●●●●●●●●

# THE NUMBER-ASSOCIATION PEG LIST REVISITED

Earlier in the book, we used the Number-Rhyme Peg List to remember the names of the founding members of the Group Theatre. In that section we also touched briefly upon the Number-Shape Peg List and the Number-Association Peg List, but didn't use them in an exercise. It's time to use the Number-Association Peg List as another technique to remember lines from a dialogue. In the list below are images that have an association to their number. In other words, the peg has some specific attribute that makes you think of the number it's linked to.

## The Number-Association Peg List

1. Unicycle
2. Bicycle
3. Tricycle
4. Car
5. Glove
6. Six-pack of soda
7. Pair of dice
8. Roller skates
9. Cat
10. Bowling

For the number one, the unicycle is the association image because a unicycle only has one wheel. For the number two, a bicycle is the association image because a bicycle has two wheels. Your association image for the number three is a tricycle because a tricycle has three wheels. Your association image for the number four is a car because a car has four wheels. Your association image for the number five is a glove because a glove has five fingers. Your association image for the number six is a six-pack of soda because a six-pack of soda has six cans. Your association image for the number seven is a pair of dice because a pair of dice is used in the game craps and you try to roll lucky number seven. Your association image for the number eight is roller skates because roller skates have eight wheels. Your association image for the number nine is a cat because a cat has nine lives. Finally, your association image for the number ten is bowling because bowling has ten frames, ten pins, and a strike has a value of ten.

We will now use the Number-Association Peg List to remember the following dialogue between a father and his daughter.

**Daughter:** Goodbye.

**Father:** Stop!
**Daughter:** What's the problem now?
**Father:** You are not leaving the house dressed like that.
**Daughter:** I'm sixteen years old. I can wear what I want.
**Father:** As long as you live under my roof, you'll live by my rules.
**Daughter:** You're the boss.
**Father:** That's right. Now go upstairs and change.
**Daughter:** You make it hard to love you, Daddy.
**Father:** You'll understand when you have kids.

Just like before, the first step is to turn the line into an image, then create a story that links that image to the Number-Association peg. Below in **(parenthesis)** are the images I've created that represent the words of the script.

Daughter: Goodbye. **(Hand waving)**
Father: Stop! **(Stop sign)**
Daughter: What's the problem now? **(Math problems)**
Father: You are not leaving the house dressed like that. **(Short skirts trapped in a house)**
Daughter: I'm sixteen years old. I can dress how I want. **(Sixteen candles in the shape of dresses on top of a cake)**
Father: As long as you live under my roof, you'll live by my rules. **(Rulers holding up a roof)**
Daughter: You're the boss. **(A mean fat boss)**
Father: That's right. Now go upstairs and change**. (Coins/loose change scattered on the right side of a staircase the entire way down)**
Daughter: You make it hard to love you, Daddy. **(A stone heart with "Daddy" written on it)**
Father: You'll understand when you have kids. **(Lots of little kids nodding their heads)**

On the next page are the stories created to help you remember this short script. As you know, if the stories presented here don't interest you, then expand or replace them with stories of your own. The sooner you work through the exercises with your own images and stories the faster you'll melt the ball of wax on top of your head.

**The Number-Association Peg for the number one is a unicycle.**
**Daughter's line: Goodbye.**
**The image that represents the line is a hand waving.**

Imagine you see a large hand riding a unicycle. There's no actual body, just a hand. The wrist is sitting on the seat and the fingers are pointed skyward. As this hand rides the unicycle, to keep his balance he waves his hand "goodbye." On the unicycle's wheel, there are twenty small hands sticking out from the tire. As the wheel goes around and around, the tiny hands look like they are waving "goodbye" too.

**The Number-Association Peg for the number two is a bicycle.**
**Father's line: Stop!**
**The image that represents the line is a stop sign.**

Imagine you're riding a bicycle, but where the wheels normally are installed are red metal stop signs. As you push down hard to pedal the bicycle, the octagonal shape of the stop signs in the front and back make the ride extremely jerky and difficult. Each time the sign lands on another one of its eight sides, you hear a crash and see sparks fly as the metal scrapes on the blacktop.

**The Number-Association Peg for the number three is a tricycle.**
**Daughter's line: What's the problem now?**
**The image that represents the line is math problems.**

Imagine a little girl riding a tricycle back and forth in front of her house. Her mother is at one end of the block and her father is at the other end. The parents each hold math problem flashcards and a bag of marshmallows. When the little girl on the tricycle gets to her mother, the mom shows her a flashcard that says $2 + 2 = ?$ The little girl rings the bell on her tricycle four times. The mother hands her a marshmallow and the little girl rides her tricycle back to her father. The father shows the little girl a flashcard that says $5 - 3 = ?$ The little girl rings the bell two times. The father hands her a marshmallow and the little girl rides her tricycle back to her mother. She continues to ride her tricycle back and forth solving math problems until the sun goes down.

**The Number-Association Peg for the number four is a car.**
**Father's line: You are not leaving the house dressed like that.**
**The image that represents the line is short skirts trapped in a house.**

Imagine a black Dodge Charger pulling into the driveway of a cute cottage style house. The driver is wearing a black leather jacket, sunglasses, and smoking a cigarette. He honks the horn and waits for his date, but she doesn't come out. The driver looks at the window of the house and sees mini-skirts flying around inside. There are red skirts and blue skirts. There are flowing flowered skirts and there are black leather skirts. But the skirts can't get out of the house. They're trapped inside. The skirts bang on the window, but the driver just sits in his car smoking his cigarette. The skirts try to break out, but they're trapped inside the house. Finally, the Dodge Charger backs down the driveway, burns his tires, and peels off down the road.

**The Number-Association Peg for the number five is a glove.**
**Daughter's line: I'm sixteen years old. I can dress how I want.**
**The image that represents the line is sixteen candles in the shape of dresses on top of a cake.**

Imagine you're at an elegant sweet sixteen party and the caterer wheels a beautiful cake into the room. The caterer is wearing the most beautiful and expensive diamond-covered gloves. You take a closer look at the cake and see a variety of uniquely shaped candles. At the top are the numbers one and six to make sixteen, but in support of the "fashion" themed party, there are sixteen candles in the shape of princess dresses and ball gowns. To light each candle, the caterer holds his diamond-studded gloves near the wicks and snaps his fingers. A tiny spark made from the diamonds scraping against each other shoots toward the candle and ignites the wicks. Once all the candles are lit, the gloves sparkle as the light from the candles reflects off of them, sending light beams across the room.

**The Number-Association Peg for the number six is a six-pack of soda.**
**Father's line: As long as you live under my roof, you'll live by my rules.**
**The image that represents the line is rulers holding up a roof.**

Imagine there's a rickety old house where you can see through holes in the paper thin walls. There's a children's party going on inside and the roof is swaying from all the running around. You take a closer look and you see that the house is very unstable because the roof is being held up by four rulers, one in each corner. The kids inside are playing a game where they see how high they can stack six-packs of soda one on top of each other. Four kids stand next to the rulers that are holding the roof up. When the whistle blows, they run to the center of the room, grab a six-pack of soda, run back to the corner, and stack one on top of the other. They measure how high their soda stack is by looking at the height on the rulers holding up the roof. Suddenly, you hear a big crash, and the cans come tumbling down. Soda sprays everywhere, and the kids dance and scream as they get soaking wet from the exploding six-packs of soda.

**The Number-Association Peg for the number seven is a pair of dice.**
**Daughter's line: You're the boss.**
**The image that represents the line is a mean fat boss.**
      Imagine you're at a craps table in Las Vegas. There's a mob of people around and you feel people pushing into your back to get a better look, which presses your belly hard against the cushion surrounding the table. Rolling the dice at the head of the table is a big, fat, mean looking man called "Boss." People say, "Great roll, Boss," or "Make it a good one, Boss." Boss has an angry scowl on his face. Boss picks up the dice, shakes them violently in his hand, and says, "Come on lucky number seven." He throws the dice and they land on four and three. Boss and the entire crowd scream, "SEVEN!!!"

**The Number-Association Peg for the number eight is roller skates.**
**Father's line: That's right. Now go upstairs and change.**
**The image that represents the line is coins/loose change scattered on the right side of a staircase the entire way down.**
      Imagine you're standing at the top of a staircase and you take a step down. You slip and realize that you put your right foot into an antique metal roller skate with metal wheels. You try to balance and step down with your left foot, but end up putting it into the left roller skate. You wobble forward and back and suddenly you slip and fall down the stairs. As you bounce and skate down the stairs, you hear clinking under the metal wheels. You look down and see thousands of quarters, dimes, nickels, and pennies scattered on the right side of the staircase. You slip on the loose change and finally grab the railing just before you crash to the floor. You balance yourself and try to kick off the roller skates, but they're stuck on your feet. You turn around and trudge back upstairs to change the roller skates out for your running shoes. The whole way up you hear the sound of metal on metal as you step on the change on the stairs.

**The Number-Association Peg for the number nine is a cat.**
**Daughter's line: You make it hard to love you, Daddy.**
**The image that represents the line is a stone heart with "Daddy" written on it.**    Imagine you see an evil looking black cat with sharp fangs gnawing violently on a stone chew toy. The angry cat is acting like a rabid dog chewing on a bone. You take a closer look and see that the cat is biting on a stone and slowly carving it into the shape of a heart. Little pieces of stone fly out of the cat's mouth as it bites down. Once the heart shape is complete, the cat chomps at the center of the stone heart and carves letters. You see the letter "D," then the letter "A," then two more "D's," and finally the letter "Y."

125

The cat licks the stone heart with "Daddy" written on it to clean off the dust and to make it smooth. With the stone heart in its mouth, the cat leaps onto the table and puts it down next to the other Father's Day gifts set out for Daddy to open when he comes home. You realize that you misinterpreted what the cat was doing and laugh at the sheer insanity of it all.

**The Number-Association Peg for the number ten is bowling.**
**Father's line: You'll understand when you have kids.**
**The image that represents the line is lots of little kids nodding their heads.**

Imagine that you're at the bowling alley and you see a kid's birthday party taking place on a few lanes. There's an old grumpy man standing in one lane looking at all the kids. He's explaining all the rules, saying, "You must roll the ball down the lane. If you throw the bowling ball, it will dent the wood and I'll throw you out of the bowling alley. Do you understand?" The group of twenty kids all nod their heads yes. The old man says, "Stay off the lanes. Do not pass the line or the buzzer will go off and I'll throw you out of the bowling alley. Do you understand?" The group of twenty kids all nod their heads yes. The old man says, "Having fun is required. You must all have fun. If you don't have fun, I'll throw you out of the bowling alley. Do you understand?" The group of twenty kids all nod their heads yes. The old man walks away and then all of the kids pick up bowling balls, hurl them down the lane, and laugh as the old man chases them around the bowling alley.

You'll notice the stories presented in this section are shorter than prior stories and they didn't contain as many details. This was done for two reasons. First, if you're able to recall the lines of this short script by first thinking about the stories above, then you're well on your way to mastering the "pegging" process. Even short stories can trigger the recollection of the information you're trying to remember if the story hits the mark in terms of being unique, not mundane, full of action, and strange enough to manufacture interest.

Second, if you struggle to remember the lines even after you retell yourself the stories, then you must expand or replace the stories presented to make them your own. As you practice the various peg lists and memory methods presented in this book, you'll become more proficient at turning your lines into images and pegging those images to one of your peg lists. You'll then be able to easily recall the lines by retelling yourself the stories that you create.

It's time now to see how well you can remember this short script. Again, don't rush. Work through the process of retelling yourself the stories. Use all your senses when you replay the story in your mind. The more vivid and real the stories are for you, the faster the lines will come back to you. Fill in the blanks below or say the answers out loud.

**The Number-Association Peg for the number one is** _____
**Daughter's line:** _____

**The Number-Association Peg for the number two is** _____
**Father's line:** _____

**The Number-Association Peg for the number three is** _____
**Daughter's line:** _____

**The Number-Association Peg for the number four is** _____
**Father's line:** _____

**The Number-Association Peg for the number five is** _____
**Daughter's line:** _____

**The Number-Association Peg for the number six is** _____
**Father's line:** _____

**The Number-Association Peg for the number seven is** _____
**Daughter's line:** _____

**The Number-Association Peg for the number eight is** _____
**Father's line:** _____

**The Number-Association Peg for the number nine is** _____
**Daughter's line:** _____

**The Number-Association Peg for the number ten is** _____
**Father's line:** _____

Turn the page to read the short script again so you can see how well you did. If you missed any lines, just go back and make the association stories for that line more bizarre so you'll ignite more interest.

**Daughter:** Goodbye.
**Father:** Stop!
**Daughter:** What's the problem now?
**Father:** You are not leaving the house dressed like that.
**Daughter:** I'm sixteen years old. I can wear what I want.
**Father:** As long as you live under my roof, you'll live by my rules.
**Daughter:** You're the boss.
**Father:** That's right. Now go upstairs and change.
**Daughter:** You make it hard to love you, Daddy.
**Father:** You'll understand when you have kids.

In this section, you learned two methods for remembering lines. It's important to note that every peg list or method here can be applied to both monologues and dialogues. Your objective should be to apply as many of these techniques as possible in the next few weeks to as many scripts as possible. Like any new hobby or skill, the more you practice, the better you'll become and the faster you'll advance your abilities. Remember that everything is taking place in your imagination, so no one will ever get hurt. Give yourself the freedom and permission to have fun and let your imagination run wild. If you feel like you need a break, go ahead and put the book down now before moving onto the next section. If you're ready to forge ahead, then turn the page.

●●●●●●●●

# SECTION 5: THE AUDITION AND CALLBACK

When you have time to prepare your monologue, creating association stories is easy because you have no time restrictions and no real pressure. But when you're thrust into a situation at an audition or callback where you're handed a script or sides to quickly memorize, then the pressure is high. Mastering the memory techniques presented in this book will help you at an audition or callback. Having superior memory skills as part of your "Actor's Toolbox" will set you apart from the other actors auditioning for the same role. When you're the only actor that the director sees who's not looking down at the sides that were just handed out, it makes you look extremely professional and well prepared. Assuming you're a good actor and a good fit for the role, these memory skills will put you in a better position to land the job.

## MEMORIZING SIDES

Sides are the few pages of a script that actors receive a day before an audition or at the audition itself. Sometimes at callbacks the actor is handed new sides or another part from the script to read. When this happens, as an actor, you have a lot of things to work on. Spending too much time trying to memorize your lines takes time away from the more important work you need to do in figuring out who you are, where you are, what you want, your relationship to the other person, how you intend to go after your objective, how you plan on overcoming any obstacles, how you feel about the situation, what technique you will use to emotionally prepare, and the creation of any character choices like physical, behavioral, and emotional traits. This is basically all an actor does to create a believable character that exists truthfully in the given circumstances. Memorizing lines needs to be done quickly, efficiently, and reliably in order to give you the freedom to really connect with the piece and the other person. Here are some secrets and suggestions for applying the memory techniques "on the fly" at an audition or callback.

# USING THE OTHER ACTOR AS YOUR PEG LIST

If you're assigned an audition partner and have time to rehearse before your turn, you might consider using the Body Peg List as your memory method. But instead of using your toes, knees, muscle, rear, etc., you should peg the images of the lines to your audition partner's body. This forces you to put all of your attention on the other person. The director and the other actor will perceive it as you truly connecting with the other person. They'll have no idea that when you're looking at their lungs you're imagining something crazy happening inside their chest. Or that when you reach over to touch their face, you're using the kinesthetic method of triggering the image of the line and the crazy story of what that image is doing to their face. Instead, it will be perceived as you having a strong emotional connection with the other person.

Again, no one needs to know how you remembered the line. It's none of their business. So long as you remember the line, what you did to recall it is completely irrelevant.

# AUDITION ROOM PEG LIST

Another tip to help you "use the space" during your audition or callback is to build a Room Peg List on the fly with the items that are actually in the room where you're auditioning. If you have the opportunity to get inside the audition room before your turn, you should be able to quickly identify objects or locations in the room that can become the pegs to which you associate the images of the lines. If time permits, you should quickly draw a picture of the room and its objects that will become your pegs.

By using the actual room attributes as your peg list, you may be able to use the space more than you normally would. You may find yourself moving more around the room to connect with the new room peg. This will appear to the director as if you're making physical choices out of an emotional subtext. They'll have no idea that you moved stage-left to the couch to help you recall a line. They'll just assume that you felt like you needed to sit down based upon your interpretation of the script. Whether or not they agree with your choice is irrelevant. The fact that you're making choices in an audition will help you stand out from most other actors.

# BLOCKING

Although blocking (the choreographed movement around the set) is normally worked on after you start rehearsals, sometimes during an audition or a callback you'll encounter a director that will give you actual blocking notes so he can see if you can take direction and see how well you utilize the space. The comments here will help you connect the blocking to the lines and to the association stories. When you're given blocking, you don't only need to know where to go next, but you must know on which line you need to move. This is especially true for film and television acting where "hitting your mark" on the right line is essential.

The method for adding blocking to the line memorization process is simply a process of layering or adding onto the association story. Let's take the Room Peg List monologue presented earlier. The piece started with, "The moon was full and the rain poured down like cats and dogs. I stood alone on the beach and watched the waves crash in the distance."

I hope you remembered those lines. We pegged the moon to the piano in the back corner of our imaginary room. We pegged the cats and dogs to the couch. We pegged standing alone to the bookcase. We pegged the crashing waves to the television. I'm confident this is all coming back to you. Imagine you were told that your blocking for these lines are for you to move to the table downstage left on the line "The moon was full" and stay there through "and the rain poured down like cats and dogs." Then imagine your instructions are to move to the chair center stage on the line "I stood alone on the beach" and stay there through "and watched the waves crash in the distance." You would layer your Room Peg List story as follows:

- Peg the image of the line "The moon was full" to the piano (remember the full moon playing the piano?)
- Then add onto the story with the downstage left table interacting with the piano and the moon. Perhaps the table stands up and walks over to the piano and starts to sing along with the moon. Or the table jumps up in the air and crashes down onto the moon. The point here is that the location where you're supposed to move to becomes another image that's layered on top of the story you created to memorize the line. We have to turn the location where we're moving to into an image and then associate it to the line and the Peg List. By adding the blocking location to the association story, it will trigger the memory of where you need to physically be when delivering the line.
- When you get to the line, "I stood alone on the beach," you're supposed to move to the chair center stage, so after you remember your story of you on the beach with the bookcase, imagine that the chair from center stage jumps up and comes flying at you and

knocks you down. Or the chair tiptoes over to you and gives you a hug. Or the chair throws its arms and legs at you. The image of the location must interact in a crazy way with you during the line that you're supposed to move on. It's sequential, meaning the blocking "add on" story happens after the story that helps you remember the line. By keeping it sequential (one after the next), you help avoid muddying the story and confusing yourself.

Since this section was short, there's no need to take a break. Let's wrap things up so you can get out there and start memorizing your lines.

●●●●●●●●

# SECTION 6:
# THE CURTAIN CALL

## BENCHMARK CHALLENGE REVISITED

You've come a very long way since you were first presented with the Benchmark Challenge at the beginning of the book. Quickly turn back to Section One (page eight) to remind yourself how many items from the list below you were able to recall before you learned the memory techniques. Now that you've mastered the Body Peg List, let's see how well you can recall the list below. Remember to tell yourself the stories as you move up from your toes. Close the book now and say all ten items of the list.

1. The Mona Lisa
2. "For Sale" sign
3. Brick building
4. The Nobel Prize
5. Two boxers with arms raised
6. Rainbow
7. Frying pan
8. Mountain
9. Hamster wheel
10. Confetti

Welcome back. I'm certain that you were able to say all ten items from the Benchmark Challenge list quickly and easily. You were asked at the beginning to not judge anything other than the results. I sincerely hope that your results have far exceeded your expectations when you first started reading this book.

We're now at the end of our memory journey together, but your adventure is just beginning. You've been empowered with proven memorization techniques that can have a profound impact on your acting career if you practice and apply them. As an actor, you should always be working to hone your craft. Mastering a process to memorize your lines quickly and creatively is yet another important skill that every actor should possess. The fact that you're reading these words means you've taken the time to work through the exercises in this book and have built a solid foundation upon which you can accelerate the memorization process.

It's important to remember the key points to these techniques. Our mind thinks in pictures, not in words, so we must turn the lines we're trying to memorize into images. Then, in order to remember something new, it must be associated to something we already know in some bizarre or interesting way. The new information we're trying to remember are the lines, and the thing that we already know are the pegs from our peg lists.

Always remember to take things slowly and to make the stories burst with action, emotion, and wackiness, so that you'll create interest in the information you're trying to recall. Finally, remember to leverage the creative being that you are as an actor and let your imagination go wherever it wants to. If you allow yourself to have fun with this process, you'll master the techniques in no time at all.

Spend the next few weeks building your peg lists. Perhaps you can create Room Peg Lists for every room in your house. You can even use the many rooms at a building you're familiar with as a Multi-Room Peg List. If you spend a lot of time at one particular theater, perhaps you can build Room Peg Lists for the parking lot, the lobby, the theater, the green room, back stage, the bathroom, the concession area, the ticket office, the lighting booth, the prop room, the stage, and so on.

You should also spend time practicing turning lines into images. The faster you can create an image that represents the line, the faster you'll be able to peg it to one of your lists. But you need to practice the techniques to improve, so get out there now and memorize something.

As mentioned earlier, if you ever have any questions about how to apply these principles, if you need any clarification of the material presented, or if you get stuck and need some guidance, I'm just an email away. I'd be glad to review your stories and help you make them even more memorable. To contact me, please either visit my website, www.jaredkelner.com, and go to the "Submit Your Peg List" section or simply email me at jared@jaredkelner.com. Be sure to tell me which peg list you're using, what you're trying to remember, and what your crazy story is. I'll review it and reply with suggestions as soon as possible.

I hope the ball of wax on top of your head that we packed full of theories, principles, and techniques has melted and that you've turned what you've learned into knowledge. Thank you for giving me the chance to share this information with you. I truly hope that it has made a positive impact on your life and I sincerely hope that you land more acting jobs because of it. If you have any positive comments about the material presented in the book or any success stories that you would like to share, please leave your comments on the website where you purchased the book or feel free to email me directly. I look forward to hearing from you soon.

●●●●●●●●

# SPECIAL OFFERS

## SPECIAL OFFER #1

The Infinite Memory Method is my ten-hour memory improvement audio training program that covers many more applications of memory techniques for your everyday life. In addition to similar peg list exercises, I go into great detail on techniques for remembering lists, names, numbers, and much more. There are four companion programs that apply the core information to sales, education, health, and food services. If you're a waiter, you'll love the food services program because I teach you how to increase your tips by remembering what people order without writing anything down. The entire program sells for $39.99 on CD and $9.99 for the audio download. As my way of saying thank you for purchasing this book, I'm happy to offer you a special gift of the entire downloadable audio program for only $6.99. If you're interested in purchasing this comprehensive memory training program, please email me at jared@jaredkelner.com and let me know you would like the secret link to the $6.99 page.

## SPECIAL OFFER #2

My first book is called *The Chamberlain Negotiation Principles: A Tale of Five Must Know Negotiation Tenets and the Insight Behind the Principles to Help You Succeed*. It is currently on the reading lists at Northeastern University; the University of Connecticut; the College of Saint Elizabeth; the University of Alaska, Fairbanks; and Barry University. I'm pleased to offer you a coupon code to purchase the book at 20% off the retail price. Go to https://www.createspace.com/3432993 and enter Discount Code: 9RPS6ZVW to receive the 20% discount.

*The Chamberlain Negotiation Principles* is a poignant business fable that explores the professional and personal impact that five critical negotiation tenets have on the lives of a struggling young salesman at the dawn of his career and an elderly subway dweller at the twilight of his self-condemned life of poverty. By weaving important negotiation tenets through a touching story as well as offering in-depth business analysis of the negotiation concepts shared in the fable, *The Chamberlain Negotiation Principles* helps you acquire a comprehensive understanding of the business process. *The Chamberlain Negotiation Principles* is a creative and valuable negotiation resource that will touch your heart and challenge your mind.

# ADDITIONAL RESOURCES

In case you're eager to learn more about memory improvement techniques from other experts in the field, the list below offers some of the best material available today. I have personally studied the material presented by these memory masters and have learned so much from them. Undoubtedly, there are more resources available than the short list of books and audio programs below, but if you want to learn more about memory improvement techniques, this list is a great place to start.

- Buzan, Tony. *The Mind Map Book: How to Use Radiant Thinking to Maximize Your Brain's Untapped Potential.* New York, NY: Penguin Group, 1993

- Buzan, Tony. *Use Your Perfect Memory: Dramatic New Techniques for Improving Your Memory-Based on the Latest Discoveries About the Human Brain.* New York, NY: Penguin Group, 1984

- Cooke, Ed. *Remember, Remember: Train Your Memory to Never Forget: Kings and Queens, British Prime Ministers, American Presidents, ... and More!* New York, NY: Penguin Group, 2008

- Foer, Joshua. *Moonwalking with Einstein: The Art and Science of Remembering Everything.* New York, NY: The Penguin Press, 2010

- Gray, Andy. *Advanced Memory Techniques: A Course in Techniques and Skills for Mentalists, Magicians and Students.* Mike Morley, 2012

- Hagwood, Scott. *Memory Power: You Can Develop a Great Memory - America's Grand Master Shows You How.* New York, NY: Free Press, A Division of Simon & Schuster, Inc., 2006

- Hancock, Jonathan. *Maximize Your Memory: Techniques and Exercises for Remembering Just About Anything.* Pleasantville, NY: Readers Digest, 2000

- Herold, Mort. *Making It Stick. Techniques For Developing a Near-Perfect Memory.* New York, NY: Bell Publishing Company, 1982

- Higbee, Kenneth L. *Your Memory: How It Works and How to Improve It.* Cambridge, MA: Da Capo Press, 2001

- Keith, Jon. *Everyday Memory Builder.* New York, NY: Berkley Books, 2001

- Keith, Jon. *Executive Memory Techniques.* New York, NY: Dell Publishing, 1989

- Lorayne, Harry. *Memory Power.* New York, NY: Harry Lorayne, 1980

- Lorayne, Harry and Lucas, Jerry. *The Memory Book: The Classic Guide to Improving Your Memory at Work, at School, and at Play.* New York, NY: Ballantine Books, 1996
- McPherson, Dr. Fiona. *The Memory Key: Unlock the Secrets to Remembering.* New York, NY: Barnes & Noble, 2004
- Minninger, Joan. *Total Recall: How to Maximize Your Memory Power.* New York, NY: MJF Books, 1997
- Nast, Jamie. *Idea Mapping: How to Access Your Hidden Brain Power, Learn Faster, Remember More, and Achieve Success in Business.* Hoboken, NJ: John Wiley & Sons, Inc., 2006
- O'Brien, Dominic. *How to Develop a Perfect Memory.* Upper Ground, London: Pavilion Books Limited, 1993
- O'Brien, Dominic. *Quantum Memory Power: Learn to Improve Your Memory with the World Memory Champion!* (Audio CD). New York, NY: Simon & Schuster Audio/Nightingale-Conant, 2003
- Trudeau, Kevin, *Mega Memory: How to Release Your Superpower Memory in 30 Minutes Or Less a Day.* New York, NY: William Morrow Paperbacks, 1997
- White, Ron, *Memory in a Month* (Audio CD). Indianapolis, IN: Ron White Publisher, 2005

# ACKNOWLEDGEMENTS

Thank you to Jamie Nast who taught me my first peg list many years ago. Thank you to all the memory experts who taught me memorization techniques that I've applied throughout my life. Thank you to Stephen Kazakoff, Piero Dusa, Javier Molina, Gerry Appel and all the acting teachers who taught me the craft of acting. Thank you to Cindy Sherwood from Second Set of Eyes (www.secondsetofeyes.com) for her editing expertise. Thank you to Rantilini S. from Rantistic (www.rantistic.zzl.org) for the fantastic cover art. Thank you to my brother Saul for creating the book's title. Thank you to my family for always supporting my passions.

# ABOUT THE AUTHOR

Jared Kelner has appeared professionally on stage and television. Jared attended The Fine and Performing Arts Center High School in Howell, New Jersey where he first studied acting. Jared then studied the Meisner technique for two years at the Duality Playhouse in New York City. After graduating cum laude with a Bachelors of Arts in Theatre from San Jose State University, Jared cofounded The Actor's Playhouse, an acting training center in Santa Clara, California. Mr. Kelner is currently teaching acting at The Playhouse Acting Academy of East Brunswick, New Jersey.

In 2006, Jared created The Infinite Mind Training Group, a memory improvement training company that offers interactive memory improvement training seminars to corporations and the general public. The Infinite Mind Training Group also offers a ten-hour comprehensive audio series on memory improvement.

In addition to Jared's acting and teaching, for over a decade he's had a successful sales career at one of the world's leading Internet corporations that designs and sells networking and communications technology.

In 2010, Jared wrote and published his first book, *The Chamberlain Negotiation Principles: A Tale of Five Must Know Negotiation Tenets and the Insight Behind the Principles to Help You Succeed*, which is currently being used at five universities.

Jared currently lives in central New Jersey. To contact him, please visit www.jaredkelner.com or email Jared at jared@jaredkelner.com.

15166853R00081

Made in the USA
Charleston, SC
20 October 2012